Copyright 2020 by Richard Wood -All rights reserved.

No part of this book may be reproduced or transmitted in any form or by any means, electronic or mechanical, including photocopying and recording, or by any information storage and retrieval system, without permission in writing from the publisher. This is a work of fiction. Names, places, characters and incidents are either the product of the author's imagination or are used fictitiously, and any resemblance to any actual persons, living or dead, organizations, events or locales is entirely coincidental. The unauthorized reproduction or distribution of this copyrighted work is ilegal.

Disclaimer Notice:

Please note the information contained within this document is for educational and entertainment purposes only. All effort has been executed to present accurate, up to date, reliable, complete information. No warranties of any kind are declared or implied. Readers acknowledge that the author is not engaged in the rendering of legal, financial, medical, or professional advice. The content within this book has been derived from various sources. Please consult a licensed professional before attempting any techniques outlined in this book.

By reading this document, the reader agrees that under no circumstances is the author responsible for any losses, direct or indirect, that are incurred as a result of the use of the information contained within this document, including, but not limited to, errors, omissions, or inaccuracies.

CONTENTS

Introduction 5
Chapter 1 Understanding the New Kitchen Appliance- Duo Crisp Air Fryer 6
    The Perks of Using the Duo Crisp Air Fryer: 6
    The Smart Working of the Dual-Functioning Instant Pot: 7
    Some Features And Specifications That You Should Know About: 8
    Safety features built within the Instant Pot: 9
    Frequently Asked Questions: 9
Chapter 2 Breakfast and brunch 10
    Brazilian Mini Turkey Pies 10
    Smoky-Sweet Air Fryer Chickpeas 11
    Sizzling Turkey Fajitas Platter 12
    Air Fried Kale Crisps 13
    Healthy Air Fryer Granola 14
    Keto Ribs 15
    Egg Frittata 16
    Air Fried Mac and Cheese 17
    Steak Kebabs 18
    Air Fryer Hard Boiled Eggs 19
    Air Fryer Hot Dogs 19
Chapter 3 Vegetarian and vegan 20
    Healthy Mediterranean Vegetables 20
    Roasted Savory Air Fryer Carrots 21
    Air Fried Quinoa 22
    Crispy Chickpeas with Ranch Seasoning 23
    Parmesan Lemon Fried Cauliflower 24
    Brussels sprouts 25
    Veggie Bake Cakes 26
    Stuffed Garlic Mushrooms 27
Chapter 4 Poultry 28
    Simple Spiced Chicken Legs 28
    Herb-Roasted Turkey Breast 29
    Crisp Chicken Casserole 30
    Fried Whole Chicken 31
    Barbecue Air Fried Chicken 32
    Boneless Air Fryer Turkey Breasts 33
    BBQ Chicken Breasts 34
    Juicy Turkey Burgers 35
    Turkey Legs 36
    Fried Chicken Tacos 37

Chapter 5 Fish and Seafood ... 38
- Coconut Shrimp ... 38
- Baked Shrimp Scampi ... 39
- Air Fryer Marinated Salmon ... 40
- Coconut Shrimp with Dip ... 41
- Air Fryer Fish ... 42
- Lobster Tails ... 43

Chapter 6 Beef Lamb And Pork ... 44
- Sweet & Sour Pork ... 44
- Air Fried Sausages ... 45
- Crispy Breaded Pork Chop ... 46
- Pigs In Blankets ... 47
- Pulled Pork Taquitos ... 48
- Sausage and Onions ... 49
- Roast Beef ... 50
- Pork Tenderloin ... 51
- Jamaican Jerk Pork ... 52
- Juicy Air Fryer Steak ... 53
- Perfect Air Fryer Pork Chops ... 54

Chapter 7 Snacks And Appetizers ... 55
- Air Fried Turkey and Fajitas ... 55
- Five Cheese Pull-Apart Bread ... 56
- Zucchini Fritters ... 57
- Air Fried Croutons ... 58
- Mini Empanadas with Chorizo ... 59
- Onion Rings ... 60
- Pizza Pasta ... 61
- Air Fried French Fries ... 62
- Air Fryer Crispy Tofu Buffalo Bites ... 63
- Curried Sweet Potato Fries With Creamy Cumin Ketchup ... 64
- Fried Hot Dogs ... 65
- Sweet Potato Chips ... 66
- Parmesan Truffle Fries ... 67
- Chicken Nuggets ... 68
- Mini Popovers ... 69
- Air Fryer Risotto Balls ... 70
- Chicken Tenders ... 71
- Chicken Empanadas ... 72
- Mozzarella Balls ... 73
- Swedish Meatballs ... 74

Stuffed Mushrooms 75
Mexican Street Style Corn on the Cob 76
Sweet and Spicy Bacon Wrapped Chicken 77
Avocado Egg Rolls 78
Sweet and Spicy Brussel Sprouts 79
Crispy Air Fried Chicken Wings 80
Air Fryer Crab Cakes 81
French Fries 82

Chapter 8 Desserts 83
Banana Bread 83
Air Fryer Brownies 84
Air Fried Cinnamon Rolls 85
Marshmallow and Chocolate Sandwiched Graham Cracker 86
Cookies and Cream Cheesecake 87
Blueberry Almond Mason Jar Cakes 88

Introduction

There are two things that are marvelous about this Instant Pot kitchen appliance. One is its diverse functionality. You can set 11 different functions on this appliance. And the other is the customizable design that turns it into an air fryer in an instant pot. Isn't it amazing that you are getting the benefits accorded by two different appliances by one?

The instant pot has a history of making such appliances which solve dual purposes for a homemaker. When not using the pressure cooker, just sway the 8-Quart lid, and you will get an excellent and efficient air fryer to try out new recipes quickly. There are 6 wet and 5 crisp cooking functions. The wet functions include pressure cook, sauté, steam, slow cook the food, sous vide, and warm your favorite dishes. The air fryer can be utilized for air frying, roasting, baking, boiling, and dehydrating. And this pretty much covers each and everything that you wish to do with your food. Furthermore, all this means that you can prepare any kind of recipe in this one appliance.

Another beautiful thing about this appliance is its design and ease of use. You need not be a soul chef or a master chef at making food. Moreover, this appliance can help you be one and that too in the comfort of your home.

All the functions on your latest Duo Crisp air fryer are customizable. You can set them right from the control panel and start preparing your favorite meals a day in and out. The delay start function deserves a special mention here. It provides the user with the added convenience of start preparing the food right on time and get it ready to serve hot. And since you are getting an air fryer, this means that there will be little to no usage of oil for preparing your food. Every kind of dish, be it your favorite chicken wings or even our everyday French fries with crispy onion rings, you can make it all in this appliance.

With this book, I aim to provide you with the correct and required knowledge about the Crisp Duo Air Fryer. Along with this, I want you to understand how it works. And why this is a great appliance to keep in your kitchen.

Chapter 1 Understanding the New Kitchen Appliance- Duo Crisp Air Fryer

The Perks of Using the Duo Crisp Air Fryer:

There are a lot of perks and benefits of using this appliance in your kitchen. Convenience, diversity, ease of use, tasty, and healthy food are only some benefits that scratch the surface. Let's know something more about how you can benefit from it.

The duality of functions facilitated by this device is something to be proud of. And looking at the control panel, you will get to know the broad scope of features that this device can perform with ease. I have been using two different appliances for pressure cooking and air frying. And let me tell you something that not even the individual appliances can perform these many functions as you are getting with this one.

Just swap the lid:

Turning your pressure cooker into an air fryer is only as hard as changing the lid. And if you would look at it, this changing of the lid transforms everything in your appliance. And to top that, you are well shielded from making any kind of mistake of mixing up the functions. Because you cannot operate the pressure cooker with the air fryer lid resting on the top of the appliance. And the same goes for when you are using it as a pressure cooker.

Placing the Lid:

The Air Fryer and Pressure cooker lid are easily locked in their place without obstructing the power cord outlet given on the appliance. The design is made to be simple and effective. And this is the case with every other Instant Pot appliance, they provide a safe and secure placement. Added to this, you will also get a separate tray to put the air fryer lid after use.

Easy to use Control Panel:

In other devices that have the same functionality or even the other Instant Pot appliances have preset functions. This literally confuses many users. But the Crisp Duo and Air Fryer do not have any such buttons to confuse you. It has just the primary function buttons provided on the front side of the pot. This time they have removed the buttons from the air fryer lid, too, and that is also something that I like about it.

Smart Accessories for a Smart Device:

Different accessories come as an add on with the Air Fryer Crisp Duo. For instance, the trivet that is made to place the food or even the pot after preparations are complete. Or, the double-layered air fryer basket is also something to be proud of with your appliance. Moreover, the multi-level air fryer basket, boiling or dehydrating tray, and the protective pad are some other essential accessories for this appliance.

One-Click Smart Functions:

Although there are no preset buttons on the appliance, you can work with some smart programs. For instance, the "Keep warm," or even the delay start button, adds another level of accessibility to the appliance.

Status Messages to your Rescue:
For a newbie, who is making their maiden attempt at cooking with the instant pot, there are status messages to help them understand their next steps. Messages like Lid, On, Off, Hot, End, Food, and Burn indicate either the completion of a process or instruct you to take some action while cooking.

All the more, this book is best for those who are looking to start cooking for the first time with such a multi-tasking appliance. You will find information about what all you can do with this appliance along with how to use it best.

The Smart Working of the Dual-Functioning Instant Pot:

Working with your Instant Pot Crisp Duo and Air Fryer is a walk in the park. I have used a lot of appliances in my kitchen, and I literally look for easier methods to prepare food. Keeping that in mind, I always look out for the functions and techniques that will help me complete everything with a minimal amount of work.

Pressure Cooker Usage:
While using the pressure cooker, always keep in mind that stainless steel lid is necessary for all kinds of pressure cooking functions. Plus, you will hear a jingle sound when the lid is locked in its place. And if not, you will see a message "Lid" being displayed on the front panel.

Steam Release Valve and Anti-Block Shield:
You will see that the steam release valve on the top of the pressure cooker lid. This release valve shall not be covered and has to be fitted every time you are using the Instant Pot pressure cooker. Other than this, the anti-block shield is installed with the valve restricts the food particles from erupting out of the pressure cooker.

Stages of Pressure Cooking:
Your food is prepared in the pressure cooker in three different stages. Starting from the pre-heating sequence, the instant pot first vaporizes the liquid in the inner pot to create the initial steam. Popping up of the float valve in this stage means that enough steam has been generated.

In the Cooking Stage, with enough pressure and steam inside the pot, the food starts to cook, and simultaneously, the timer will start. When cooking is complete, there is Depressurization. In this stage, you can either set the "Keep Warm" function and set the timer until you are ready to serve the food, or the sequence will end with a message displayed on the small screen.

Other than this, set procedure for cooking, you can also set up the smart functions to help you sauté, slow cook, and sous vide your food.

Air Frying and how it works:
Air Frying is an excellent way to bring out that lip-smacking flavor in your food without compromising its integrity. Air frying with this appliance can be done in three types of bases. One is the multi-level air fryer basket. Secondly, you can use any oven-safe cookware which fits inside the pot. And thirdly, you can put the food directly inside the pot.

There are different functions that you can choose with air frying, roasting is best for beef, lamb, pork, and other poultry products. It takes around 40 minutes to roast your food in the air fryer.

The baking functions transform your Instant pot air fryer into an oven for baking purposes. Cakes, pastries, buns, and other such food items can be easily prepared within 30 minutes.

For Broiling, the air fryer distributes heat from the top all the way down. That is why it is better if you would place the food items closer to the heating element for broiling purposes. Typically, a broiling sequence takes around 8 minutes to complete.

For Dehydrating, you need to make sure that there is enough space between the food items to let the air pass through. In other terms, this book will help you solve various problems while you are cooking or preparing your food.

In everyday cooking, these small things like dehydrating and sauté matter a lot. That is why you will need this book to help you with such functions and understand their scope.

Some Features And Specifications That You Should Know About:

The Instant Pot Crisp Duo and Air Fryer is a smart device, there is no doubt in that. Added to this, there are a few other things that make it a better choice over other such appliances. And these can further convince you to add it to your kitchen appliance inventory.

Intuitive Control Panel:

Starting with the control panel, you already know that it can help you perform up to 11 functions with your instant pot. At the same time, you can also fix your desired temperature and timer from the control panel too. You can increase the timer in increments of 5 minutes and temperature in increments of 1 degree.

Smart Programs:

There are a few intelligent programs that can also be set on the instant pot. This includes putting the pressure cooker or the air fryer on Standby Mode. Plus, you can also turn the sound off or on at your wish from the same control panel. The Delay start and Keep Warm functions are also some good and useful functions that you can work within the instant pot.

Ease of Clean:

Since you can remove most of the bigger parts from the instant pot, it is easier to clean and make sure that it stays clean. While using the appliance, make sure that you clean it before use and also do the same after you have used it.

Deep-fried texture without using much oil:

One of the greatest bonuses of using an air fryer is that you will get to eat crispy and deep-fried food without using oil. That is the real beauty of an air fryer. With the instant pot, there is, however, an add-on. The food fried in it will also have a golden finish, which further enhances your food's quality and finish.

Specifications:

The Instant Pot Crisp Duo and Air Fryer works with 1500 watts of power and weighs around 22 lb. It is 14 inches long, 13.5 inches wide, and stands at 15 inches of height. The 8-quart lid sized instant pot is suitably large to place anywhere in your kitchen without taking up too much space.

Safety features built within the Instant Pot:

- When the pressure cooker is fully pressurized, you cannot open the lid until and unless the pressure is released. This feature has been incorporated to protect you from harm or damage due to an abrupt release of the lid forcefully.
- Another good thing is that you cannot start cooking if the lid is not locked in its set place. Added to it, you will see a message "Lid" being displayed on the control panel.
- There is a smart safety function that won't let the temperature go beyond a limit. These limitations are further set as per the program you have opted for preparing the dish.
- The food items may get stuck at the bottom, or there is not enough liquid in the pot for the pressure cooker. In that case, there is overheating. To prevent any kind of damage, there is an overheating protection sequence that limits the formation of excessive heat.
- The Instant Pot has an automatic pressure control system which maintains the pressure and suspends heating if the pressure inside the pot is more than the desired level.

There are features, specifications, and an introduction to the significant aspects of this book that you would want to know about. Other than this, you will get to read around 80 recipes that you can prepare with this appliance. Some of these recipes can be prepared with the pressure cooker and others with the air fryer. All of them are divided into different meal courses and kinds to help further you decide what you can eat for the morning breakfast, or evening snacks, or even for dinner.

Frequently Asked Questions:

1. How Can I assure that there is enough liquid inside the pot for pressure cooking?

Most of the time, you will get the required levels of liquid indicated in the recipe instructions you are following. If not, then make sure that you put in enough water in the pot as it is stated on the inside of the container.

2. Can I use the 6 Quart Lid on the 8 Quart pot?

No, this is not feasible, let alone safe. Interchanging different parts or lids can lead to improper sealing or locking, thus making you and the appliance vulnerable.

3. Can I change the Program settings once the cooking has started?

Yes, you can change the temperature and time settings as per your requirements, even in the middle of cooking.

4. What is the right time to open up the Pressure Cooker lid?

The Pressure Cooker lid has to be opened with the utmost care and diligence. When you want to open the lid, first make sure that all the pressure has been released, and the float valve is in the down position. Also, do not try to force open the lid. If it is not easily disassembled from its position, there may be some pressure still left inside, make sure to release it first and then open the lid.

Chapter 2 Breakfast and brunch

Brazilian Mini Turkey Pies

Prep time: 2 minutes, cook time: 10 minutes; Serves 8

10 Ingredients
8 Slices Filo Pastry
1.76oz Shredded Turkey
1 Small Egg beated
1.6oz ml Coconut Milk
1.6oz Whole Milk
7 oz Homemade Tomato Sauce
1 oz Turkey Stock
1 Tsp Oregano
1 Tbsp Coriander
Salt & Pepper

Instructions
1. Place your wet ingredients into a mixing bowl apart from the egg and mix well.
2. You will now have a pale looking sauce that will be the stock for your pie. Add the turkey and seasoning and mix again. Put to one side.
3. Line your little pie cases with a little flour to stop them sticking and then line with the filo pastry. Aim for one sheet of filo for each pie you are doing and have it centered so that you can then fold over the spare pastry for the top of the pie.
4. Add the mixture to each mini pie pot so that they are ¾ full.
5. Cover the top with the remaining pastry and then brush the egg along the top.
6. Place them into the Instant Pot Duo Crisp Air Fryer Basket.
7. Close the Air Fryer lid and cook for ten minutes at 350°F.

Nutrition Facts Per Serving
Calories 47, Total Fat 3g, Total Carbs 3g, Protein 2g

Smoky-Sweet Air Fryer Chickpeas

Prep time: 5 minutes, cook time: 16 minutes; Serves 4

6 Ingredients
1 (15 ounces) can chickpeas
2 tablespoons aquafaba from chickpeas
1 tablespoon maple syrup
2 teaspoons smoked paprika
1 1/2 teaspoons garlic powder
1/2 teaspoon sea salt

Instructions
1. Drain the chickpeas while reserving aquafaba obtained. Don't rinse chickpeas.
2. Add chickpeas to the Instant Pot Duo Crisp Air Fryer basket, shake to a single layer, place inside the Air Fryer. Choose the Air Fry function and close the lid.
3. Air Fry at 390°F for at least 8 minutes.
4. While the chickpeas cook, whisk together 2 tablespoons aquafaba, maple syrup, smoked paprika, garlic powder, and salt in a mixing bowl (Save the remaining aquafaba for further use.)
5. Add chickpeas fresh from the Instant Pot Duo Crisp Air Fryer and stir to coat them completely. Return the flavored chickpeas to the air fryer basket and using a spatula to get every last bit of the sauce.
6. Return chickpeas to the Instant Pot Duo Crisp Air Fryer. Air Fry at 390°F for 5 more minutes. Shake the basket, return to the Fryer for another 3-5 minutes, until chickpeas are crisp.
7. Transfer to a serving bowl. Serve warm or at room temperature.

Nutrition Facts Per Serving
Calories 410, Total Fat 6g, Total Carbs 69g, Protein 20g

Sizzling Turkey Fajitas Platter

Prep time: 5 minutes, cook time: 20 minutes; Serves 2

13 Ingredients
6 Tortilla Wraps
3.5oz Leftover Turkey Breast
1 Large Avocado
1 Large Yellow Pepper
1 Large Red Pepper
1 Large Green Pepper
½ Small Red Onion
5 Tbsp Soft Cheese
3 Tbsp Cajun Spice
2 Tbsp Mexican Seasoning
1 Tsp Cumin
Salt & Pepper
1/2 cup Fresh Coriander

Instructions
1. Start by slicing the salad. Chop the avocado to little wedges. Dice the red onion. Slice the peppers into thin slices.
2. Chop up the turkey breast into small little chunks.
3. Place the turkey, peppers, and onions into a bowl and mix with all the seasonings along with the soft cheese and then place in silver foil.
4. Place all of them in Instant Pot Duo Crisp Air Fryer tray and then close the lid.
5. Select the Air Fry option. Cook for 20 minutes at 390°F.
6. Once done, serve them hot.

Nutrition Facts Per Serving
Calories 647, Total Fat 39g, Total Carbs 44g, Protein 30g

Air Fried Kale Crisps

Prep time: 10 minutes, cook time: 10 minutes; Serves 2-4

4 Ingredients
1 bunch Tuscan kale, stems and ribs removed, leaves cut into 2-inch (5-cm) pieces
2 Tbsp. olive oil
1/2 tsp. kosher salt, plus more, to taste
1/4 tsp. freshly ground pepper

Instructions
1. Preheat Instant Pot Duo Crisp Air Fryer to 390°F.
2. In a large bowl, toss together kale, olive oil, 1/2 tsp. salt, and pepper.
3. In batches, place the kale in the air fry basket and insert it into the Instant Pot Duo Crisp Air Fryer. Cook until the kale gets crisp, about 5 minutes.
4. Transfer the chips to a bowl and season with salt. Serve warm or at room temperature.

Nutrition Facts Per Serving
Calories 75.4, Total Fat 7g, Total Carbs 2.3g, Protein 0.8g

Healthy Air Fryer Granola

Prep time: 5 minutes, cook time: 15 minutes; Serves 8

18 Ingredients
2 cup Rolled Oats
1/2 cup Toasted Wheat Germ
1/4 cup Dried Cherries
1/8 cup Dried Cranberries
1/4 cup Dried Blueberries
1/8 cup Pepitas
1/8 cup Sunflower Seeds
1 Tbsp Flaxseed
1/8 cup Chopped pecans
1/8 cup Chopped Almonds
1/8 cup Chopped Walnuts
1/8 cup Chopped Hazelnuts.
2 tbsp Honey or Agave Extract
1/2 tsp Vanilla extract
1/4 cup Maple Syrup
6 tbsp Olive Oil
1/2 tsp Ground Cinnamon
1/8 tsp Ground Cloves

Instructions
1. Combine all the dry ingredients in a large or a medium bowl.
2. Mix the agave or honey with the oil and maple syrup.
3. Thoroughly mix the syrup mix with the dry ingredients, stirring well to fully coat all of the ingredients.
4. Choose the Air Fry option from the Instant Pot Duo Crisp Air Fryer and set the temperature to 350°F. Press start and let it preheat.
5. Add the food to the Air Fryer and Air Fry at 350°F for 15 minutes, stirring every 5 minutes until the granola is golden brown.
6. Let it cool and store for up to three weeks in an airtight container

Nutrition Facts Per Serving
Calories 351, Total Fat 19g, Total Carbs 38g, Protein 7g

Keto Ribs

Prep time: 10 minutes, cook time: 35 minutes; Serves 6

4 Ingredients

3.5 lbs pork baby back ribs about 2 racks of ribs
1/3 cup spicy dry rub
1/2 cup Keto BBQ sauce
1 cup Zevia Cola or Chicken Broth

Instructions

1. Season the pork ribs on the both sides with the dry rub.
2. Marinate the ribs for at least 4 hours.
3. Set the ribs in the Instant Pot Duo Crisp Air Fryer.
4. Pour the chicken broth or keto-friendly Cola soda at the bottom of the pot.
5. Close the Air Fryer lid and cook the ribs for 25-30 minutes at 390°F.
6. Place them into the Instant Pot Duo Crisp Air Fryer Basket.
7. Top the ribs with BBQ sauce.
8. Select the option Air Fryer.
9. Close the Air Fryer lid and cook for about 5 minutes.

Nutrition Facts Per Serving

Calories 379, Total Fat 27g, Total Carbs 3g, Protein 31g

Egg Frittata

Prep time: 10 minutes, cook time: 15 minutes; Serves 2

10 Ingredients

4 eggs
½ cup milk
2 green onions chopped
¼ cup baby Bella mushrooms chopped
¼ cup spinach chopped
¼ cup red bell pepper chopped
¼ cup cheddar cheese
½ tsp salt
½ tsp black pepper
Dash of hot sauce

Instructions

1. Grease a 6x3 inch round or square pan with butter and set it aside.
2. Whisk the eggs and milk in a large bowl until they are thoroughly blended. Stir in green onions, mushrooms, salt, black pepper, spinach, red bell pepper, cheddar cheese, and hot sauce.
3. Pour the egg mixture into a greased pan.
4. Place in the Instant Pot Duo Crisp Air Fryer and close the lid. Cook on 360°F for 15-18 minutes, or until a toothpick comes out clean.

Nutrition Facts Per Serving

Calories 227, Total Fat 15g, Total Carbs 6g, Protein 17g

Air Fried Mac and Cheese

Prep time: 10 minutes, cook time: 35 minutes; Serves 4

6 Ingredients

1 cup Elbow Macaroni
1/2 cup Broccoli or Cauliflower (equal size small florets)
1/2 cup Milk (Warmed)
1 1/2 cup Cheddar Cheese (grated)
Salt and Pepper
1 tbsp Parmesan Cheese (grated)

Instructions

1. Preheat the Instant Pot Duo Crisp Air Fryer at 390°F.
2. Boil some water over high heat, and reduce the heat to med and add macaroni & vegetables.
3. Simmer it until macaroni is al dente & vegetables are tender but not mushy (for about 7-10 minutes). Drain the vegetables and pasta, & return them to the basket.
4. Add Cheddar cheese and milk to the macaroni and vegetables, and toss to combine. Season with pepper and salt.
5. Pour pasta mixture into an ovenproof dish. Then sprinkle the Parmesan cheese over top of it.
6. Place the dish onthe Instant Pot Duo Crisp Air Fryer Basket and adjust the temperature at 350°F.
7. Close the Air Fryer lid and cook for bake it for fifteen minutes (the pasta will be bubbling).
8. Allow it to sit for 5-10 minutes in the Instant Pot Duo Crisp Air Fryer before serving.

Nutrition Facts Per Serving

Calories 291, Total Fat 16.5g, Total Carbs 18.8g, Protein 16.9g

Steak Kebabs

Prep time: 10 minutes, cook time: 12 minutes; Serves 4

11 Ingredients

1 lb sirloin steak cut into 1-inch chunks
¼ cup olive oil
¼ cup of soy sauce
1 Tbsp garlic minced
1 tsp brown sugar
½ tsp ground cumin
¼ tsp black pepper
8 oz Baby Bella mushrooms stem removed
1 red onion chopped into 1-inch pieces
1 Green Bell Pepper chopped into 1-inch pieces
salt and pepper to taste

Instructions

1. Mix together soy sauce, garlic, cumin, salt, steak, olive oil, and black pepper. Allow marinating for around 30 minutes.
2. While preparing for cooking, select the Air Fry option. Adjust the temperature to 390°F and press start to begin preheating.
3. Once the preheating temperature is reached, place the marinated meat, baby Bella mushrooms, green pepper, and red onion on the Instant Pot Duo Crisp Air Fryer tray.
4. Place the tray inside of Instant Pot Duo Crisp Air fryer. Air Fry for 10-12 minutes while flipping halfway.

Nutrition Facts Per Serving

Calories 310, Total Fat 18g, Total Carbs 9g, Protein 28g

Air Fryer Hard Boiled Eggs

Prep time: 1 minute, cook time: 15 minutes; Serves 3

1 Ingredients

6 large eggs

Instructions

1. Select the Air Fry option on the Instant Pot Duo Crisp Air Fryer. Adjust the temperature to 390°F and press start to begin preheating.
2. Once the preheating is complete, place the eggs on the Air Fryer tray in the Air Fryer basket and close the lid. Air Fry on 300°F for 15 minutes. Once the set time is over, remove the eggs from the Instant Pot Duo Crisp Air Fryer tray and place them in a bowl filled with ice water for 5 minutes.
3. Remove and peel the eggs for eating.

Nutrition Facts Per Serving

Calories 56, Total Fat 4g, Total Carbs 0g, Protein 5g

Air Fryer Hot Dogs

Prep time: 2 minutes, cook time: 8 minutes; Serves 6

1 Ingredients

6 Hot Dogs

6 Hot Dog Buns

Instructions

1. Simply place the hot dogs in the Instant Pot Duo Crisp Air Fryer basket and close the lid. Select the Air Fry option and Air Fry on 400°F for 4-6 minutes. Remove the hot dogs and put them in buns. Place them back in Air Fryer basket and cook on 400°F for two more minutes.
2. Remove and top with your favorite toppings.

Nutrition Facts Per Serving

Calories 228, Total Fat 8g, Total Carbs 30g, Protein 9g

Chapter 3 Vegetarian and vegan

Healthy Mediterranean Vegetables

Prep time: 5 minutes, cook time: 20 minutes; Serves 4

11 Ingredients

1.76oz Cherry Tomatoes
1 Large Courgette
1 Green Pepper
1 Large Parsnip
1 Medium Carrot
1 Tsp Mixed Herbs
2 Tbsp Honey
1 Tsp Mustard
2 Tsp Garlic Puree
6 Tbsp Olive Oil
Salt & Pepper

Instructions

1. At the bottom of your Air Fryer slice up the courgette and green pepper and place them into the Instant Pot Duo Crisp Air Fryer Tray. Peel and dice the parsnip and carrot and add the cherry tomatoes whole while still on the vine for extra flavor.
2. Drizzle it with 3 tablespoons of olive oil
3. Close the Air Fryer lid and cook for 15 minutes at 350°F.
4. In the meantime, mix up the rest of your ingredients and place them into an Air Fryer basket.
5. When the vegetables are done transfer them from the tray of the Air Fryer into the basket and shake well so that all the vegetables are covered in the marinade.
6. Sprinkle it with a little more salt and pepper and place them into Instant Pot Duo Crisp Air Fryer.
7. Close the Air Fryer lid and cook for 5 minutes on 390°F.

Nutrition Facts Per Serving

Calories 281, Total Fat 21g, Total Carbs 21g, Protein 2g

Roasted Savory Air Fryer Carrots

Prep time: 10 minutes, cook time: 20 minutes; Serves 4

7 Ingredients

1 lb medium-sized carrots washed and peeled
2 Tbsp olive oil
1/4 cup grated parmesan cheese
Salt and pepper to taste
½ tsp garlic powder
½ tsp paprika
Fresh chopped parsley

Instructions

1. In a large bowl, Place the carrots and toss them with olive oil, garlic powder, and paprika.
2. Place on the tray and in the Instant Pot Duo Crisp Air Fryer basket. Close the Instant Pot Duo Crisp Air Fryer lid and choose the Air Fry option. Cook on 380°F for 20 minutes, shaking halfway through or stirring for uniform cooking.
3. Once it is done, top with parmesan cheese and parsley. Salt and pepper to taste.

Nutrition Facts Per Serving

Calories 126, Total Fat 6g, Total Carbs 17g, Protein 1g

Air Fried Quinoa

Prep time: 20 minutes, cook time: 21 minutes; Serves 4

2 Ingredients

2 cups quinoa
2 cups of water

Instructions

1. In a fine-mesh sieve, rinse quinoa.
2. Place them into the Instant Pot Duo Crisp Air Fryer Basket.
3. Close the Air Fryer lid and cook for about 5 minutes.
4. Stir it well and add 2 cups of water.
5. Close the Air Fryer lid again and cook for about 2 more minutes.
6. Using a fork, fluff the quinoa, and serve immediately or place it into freezer bags for long-term freezer storage.

Nutrition Facts Per Serving

Calories 159, Total Fat 3g, Total Carbs 27g, Protein 6g

Crispy Chickpeas with Ranch Seasoning

Prep time: 2 minutes, cook time: 20 minutes; Serves 2

3 Ingredients

15 oz chickpeas (1 can 15 oz)also known as garbanzo beans
1 tsp olive oil
1 tbsp dry ranch seasoning mix

Instructions

1. Drain & rinse the chickpeas and dry them thoroughly with a kitchen towel.
2. Spread chickpeas evenly on one Instant Pot Duo Crisp Air Fryer Tray.
3. Place the tray inside the Instant Pot Duo Crisp Air Fryer. Select the option Air Fryer.
4. Close the Air Fryer lid and cook for about 17 minutes at 390°F.
5. Stir the chickpeas after it is cooked.
6. Immediately remove and toss with ranch seasoning. Serve hot or cold.

Nutrition Facts Per Serving

Calories 263, Total Fat 4.8g, Total Carbs 48.1g, Protein 10.5g

Parmesan Lemon Fried Cauliflower

Prep time: 5 minutes, cook time: 20 minutes; Serves 4

13 Ingredients

15 oz chickpeas
1 tsp olive oil
1 lb head of cauliflower cut into florets
1/2 tsp salt
1/4 tsp freshly ground pepper
Lemon slices for garnish
Sauce Mixture ingredients:
1/4 cup olive oil
1/4 cup finely grated Parmesan cheese preferably Parmigiano Reggiano
1 tbsp finely chopped parsley
1 tbsp lemon juice
1 tsp lemon zest
Salt and freshly ground pepper to taste
Salt and freshly ground pepper to taste

Instructions

1. In a big bowl, combine the cauliflower, olive oil, salt, and pepper. Toss to coat evenly.
2. Place them into the Instant Pot Duo Crisp Air Fryer Basket.
3. Select the option Air Fryer. Close the Air Fryer lid and cook for about 15 minutes at 400°F.
4. Stir after it gets cooked.
5. Meanwhile, in a medium bowl combine Sauce Mixture ingredients.
6. Serve hot topped with prepared sauce.

Nutrition Facts Per Serving

Calories 457, Total Fat 9.9g, Total Carbs 67.6g, Protein 24.3g

Brussels sprouts

Prep time: 5 minutes, cook time: 10 minutes; Serves 2

4 Ingredients

2 cups Brussels sprouts – sliced lengthwise into 1/4" thick pieces
1 tablespoon olive oil or maple syrup
1 tablespoon balsamic vinegar
1/4 teaspoon sea salt

Instructions

1. In a bowl, toss together the oil or maple syrup, Brussels, vinegar, and salt.
2. Place them into the Instant Pot Duo Crisp Air Fryer Basket.
3. Close the Air Fryer lid and cook at 400°F for 8-10 minutes, stir it after 5 minutes and then at again at the 8 minute mark.
4. Make sure they are for crispy and browned, but not burnt!

Nutrition Facts Per Serving

Calories 72, Total Fat 7.1g, Total Carbs 1.6g, Protein 0.5g

Veggie Bake Cakes

Prep time: 2 minutes, cook time: 12 minutes; Serves 2

2 Ingredients

Leftover Vegetable Bake
1 Tbsp Plain Flour

Instructions

1. Preheat the Instant Pot Duo Crisp Air Fryer at 350°F.
2. Mix the flour with the leftover vegetable bake. It will now become a thick dough.
3. Place them into the Instant Pot Duo Crisp Air Fryer Basket.
4. Close the Air Fryer lid and cook for 12 minutes on 350°F.
5. Serve hot.

Nutrition Facts Per Serving

Calories 37, Total Fat 3g, Total Carbs 2g, Protein 0.4g

Stuffed Garlic Mushrooms

Prep time: 10 minutes, cook time: 25 minutes; Serves 4

7 Ingredients

6 Small Mushrooms
0.7oz Onion peeled and diced
1 Tbsp Breadcrumbs
1 Tsp Garlic Puree
1 Tbsp Olive Oil
1 Tsp Parsley
Salt & Pepper

Instructions

1. In a bowl, mix together garlic, breadcrumbs, olive oil, onion, parsley, salt, and pepper. Make sure they are mixed thoroughly.
2. Clean the mushrooms and remove the middle stalks. Fill the middle area with your breadcrumb mixture.
3. Place them into the Instant Pot Duo Crisp Air Fryer Basket.
4. Close the Air Fryer lid and cook the mushrooms on a 350°F heat for 10 minutes and then serve.

Nutrition Facts Per Serving

Calories 43, Total Fat 3g, Total Carbs 3g, Protein 1g

Chapter 4 Poultry

Simple Spiced Chicken Legs

Prep time: 5 minutes, cook time: 25 minutes; Serves 6

7 Ingredients

2-2.5 lbs chicken drumsticks 6-8 legs
2 tbsp olive oil
1 tsp kosher salt
1 tsp pepper
1 tsp garlic powder
1 tsp smoked paprika
1/2 tsp cumin

Instructions

1. Take a large bowl and drizzle the drumsticks with olive oil and toss them to coat.
2. Take a small bowl, stir together the remaining ingredients followed by sprinkling over drumsticks and toss to coat evenly.
3. Divide the coated chicken onto cooking trays of the Instant Pot Duo Crisp Air Fryer.
4. Select Air Fry from the display panel, then adjust the temperature to 400°F and the time to 25 minutes, touch the start button.
5. Once preheated, insert two cooking trays in the top-most position and in the bottom-most position one in each.
6. After half time, turn the food over and switch the cooking trays between the top and bottom positions.
7. When the Air Fryer program is complete, check to make sure the thickest portion of the meat reads at least 165°F.
8. Remove and serve hot.

Nutrition Facts Per Serving

Calories 222, Total Fat 14g, Total Carbs 1g, Protein 23g

Herb-Roasted Turkey Breast

Prep time: 10 minutes, cook time: 60 minutes; Serves 8

10 Ingredients

3 lb turkey breast

Rub Ingredients

2 tbsp olive oil
2 tbsp lemon juice
1 tbsp minced Garlic
2 tsp ground mustard
2 tsp kosher salt
1 tsp pepper
1 tsp dried rosemary
1 tsp dried thyme
1 tsp ground sage

Instructions

1. Take a small bowl and thoroughly combine the Rub Ingredients in it. Rub this on the outside of the turkey breast and under any loose skin.
2. Place the coated turkey breast keeping skin side up on a cooking tray.
3. Place the drip pan at the bottom of the cooking chamber of the Instant Pot Duo Crisp Air Fryer. Select Air Fry option, post this, adjust the temperature to 360°F and the time to one hour, then touch start.
4. When preheated, add the food to the cooking tray in the lowest position. Close the lid for cooking.
5. When the Air Fry program is complete, check to make sure that the thickest portion of the meat reads at least 160°F, remove the turkey and let it rest for 10 minutes before slicing and serving.

Crisp Chicken Casserole

Prep time: 5 minutes, cook time: 15 minutes; Serves 4

14 Ingredients

3 cup chicken, shredded
12 oz bag egg noodles
1/2 large onion
1/2 cup chopped carrots
1/4 cup frozen peas
1/4 cup frozen broccoli pieces
2 stalks celery chopped
5 cup chicken broth
1 tsp garlic powder
salt and pepper to taste
1 cup cheddar cheese, shredded
1 package French's onions
1/4 cup sour cream
1 can cream of chicken and mushroom soup

Instructions

1. Place the chicken, vegetables, garlic powder, salt and pepper, and broth and stir. Then place it into the Instant Pot Duo Crisp Air Fryer Basket.
2. Press or lightly stir the egg noodles into the mix until damp/wet.
3. Select the option Air Fryer and cook for 4 minutes.
4. Stir in the sour cream, can of soup, cheese, and 1/3 of the French's onions.
5. Top with the remaining French's onions and close the Air Fryer lid and cook for about 10 more minutes.

Nutrition Facts Per Serving

Calories 301, Total Fat 17g, Total Carbs 17g, Protein 20g

Fried Whole Chicken

Prep time: 5 minutes, cook time: 70 minutes; Serves 4

8 Ingredients

1 Whole chicken
2 Tbsp or spray of oil of choice
1 tsp garlic powder
1 tsp onion powder
1 tsp paprika
1 tsp Italian seasoning
2 Tbsp Montreal Steak Seasoning (or salt and pepper to taste)
1.5 cup chicken broth

Instructions

1. Truss and wash the chicken.
2. Mix the seasoning and rub a little amount on the chicken.
3. Pour the broth inside the Instant Pot Duo Crisp Air Fryer.
4. Place the chicken in the air fryer basket.
5. Select the option Air Fry and Close the Air Fryer lid and cook for 25 minutes.
6. Spray or rub the top of the chicken with oil and rub it with half of the seasoning.
7. Close the air fryer lid and air fry again at 400°F for 10 minutes.
8. Flip the chicken, spray it with oil, and rub with the remaining seasoning.
9. Again air fry it for another ten minutes.
10. Allow the chicken to rest for 10 minutes.

Nutrition Facts Per Serving

Calories 436, Total Fat 28g, Total Carbs 4g, Protein 42g

Barbecue Air Fried Chicken

Prep time: 5 minutes, cook time: 26 minutes; Serves 10

10 Ingredients

1 teaspoon Liquid Smoke
2 cloves Fresh Garlic smashed
1/2 cup Apple Cider Vinegar
3 pounds Chuck Roast well-marbled with intramuscular fat
1 Tablespoon Kosher Salt
1 Tablespoon Freshly Ground Black Pepper
2 teaspoons Garlic Powder
1.5 cups Barbecue Sauce
1/4 cup Light Brown Sugar + more for sprinkling
2 Tablespoons Honey optional and in place of 2 TBL sugar

Instructions

1. Add meat to the Instant Pot Duo Crisp Air Fryer Basket, spreading out the meat.
2. Select the option Air Fry.
3. Close the Air Fryer lid and cook at 300 degrees F for 8 minutes. Pause the Air Fryer and flip meat over after 4 minutes.
4. Remove the lid and baste with more barbecue sauce and sprinkle with a little brown sugar.
5. Again Close the Air Fryer lid and set the temperature at 400°F for 9 minutes. Watch meat though the lid and flip it over after 5 minutes.

Nutrition Facts Per Serving

Calories 360, Total Fat 16g, Total Carbs 27g, Protein 27g

Boneless Air Fryer Turkey Breasts

Prep time: 10 minutes, cook time: 50 minutes; Serves 4

6 Ingredients

3 lb boneless breast
¼ cup mayonnaise
2 tsp poultry seasoning
1 tsp salt
½ tsp garlic powder
¼ tsp black pepper

Instructions

1. Choose the Air Fry option on the Instant Pot Duo Crisp Air fryer. Set the temperature to 360°F and push start. The preheating will start.
2. Season your boneless turkey breast with mayonnaise, poultry seasoning, salt, garlic powder, and black pepper.
3. Once preheated, Air Fry the turkey breasts on 360°F for 1 hour, turning every 15 minutes or until internal temperature has reached a temperature of 165°F.

Nutrition Facts Per Serving

Calories 558, Total Fat 18g, Total Carbs 1g, Protein 98g

BBQ Chicken Breasts

Prep time: 5 minutes, cook time: 15 minutes; Serves 4

Ingredients

4 boneless skinless chicken breast about 6 oz each
1-2 Tbsp bbq seasoning

Instructions

1. Cover both sides of chicken breast with the BBQ seasoning. Cover and marinate the in the refrigerator for 45 minutes.
2. Choose the Air Fry option and set the temperature to 400°F. Push start and let it preheat for 5 minutes.
3. Upon preheating, place the chicken breast in the Instant Pot Duo Crisp Air Fryer basket, making sure they do not overlap. Spray with oil.
4. Cook for 13-14 minutes, flipping halfway.
5. Remove chicken when the chicken reaches an internal temperature of 160°F. Place on a plate and allow to rest for 5 minutes before slicing.

Nutrition Facts Per Serving

Calories 131, Total Fat 3g, Total Carbs 2g, Protein 24g

Juicy Turkey Burgers

Prep time: 5 minutes, cook time: 25 minutes; Serves 8

8 Ingredients

1 lb ground turkey 85% lean / 15% fat
¼ cup unsweetened apple sauce
½ onion grated
1 Tbsp ranch seasoning
2 tsp Worcestershire Sauce
1 tsp minced garlic
¼ cup plain breadcrumbs
Salt and pepper to taste

Instructions

1. Combine the onion, ground turkey, unsweetened apple sauce, minced garlic, breadcrumbs, ranch seasoning, Worchestire sauce, and salt and pepper. Mix them with your hands until well combined. Form 4 equally sized hamburger patties with them.
2. Place these burgers in the refrigerator for about 30 minutes to have them firm up a bit.
3. While preparing for cooking, select the Air Fry option. Set the temperature of 360°F and the cook time as required. Press start to begin preheating.
4. Once the preheating temperature is reached, place the burgers on the tray in the Air fryer basket, making sure they don't overlap or touch. Cook on for 15 minutes, flipping halfway through.

Nutrition Facts Per Serving

Calories 183, Total Fat 3g, Total Carbs 11g, Protein 28g

Turkey Legs

Prep time: 5 minutes, cook time: 40 minutes; Serves 2

6 Ingredients
2 large turkey legs
1 1/2 tsp smoked paprika
1 tsp brown sugar
1 tsp season salt
½ tsp garlic powder
oil for spraying avocado, canola, etc.

Instructions
1. Mix the smoked paprika, brown sugar, seasoned salt, garlic powder thoroughly.
2. Wash and pat dry the turkey legs.
3. Rub the made seasoning mixture all over the turkey legs making sure to get under the skin also.
4. While preparing for cooking, select the Air Fry option. Press start to begin preheating.
5. Once the preheating temperature is reached, place the turkey legs on the tray in the Instant Pot Duo Crisp Air Fryer basket. Lightly spray them with oil.
6. Air Fry the turkey legs on 400°F for 20 minutes. Then, open the Air Fryer lid and flip the turkey legs and lightly spray with oil. Close the Instant Pot Duo Crisp Air Fryer lid and cook for 20 more minutes.
7. Remove and Enjoy.

Nutrition Facts Per Serving
Calories 958, Total Fat 46g, Total Carbs 3g, Protein 133g

Fried Chicken Tacos

Prep time: 10 minutes, cook time: 10 minutes; Serves 4

24 Ingredients

Chicken

1 lb. chicken tenders or breast chopped into 2-inch pieces
1 tsp garlic powder
½ tsp onion powder
1 large egg
1 ½ tsp salt
1 tsp paprika
3 Tbsp buttermilk
¾ cup All-purpose flour
3 Tbsp corn starch

Spicy Mayo

½ tsp salt
¼ cup mayonnaise
1 tsp garlic powder

½ tsp black pepper
½ tsp cayenne pepper
oil for spraying

Coleslaw

¼ tsp red pepper flakes
2 cups coleslaw mix
1 Tbsp brown sugar
½ tsp salt
2 Tbsp apple cider vinegar
1 Tbsp water

2 Tbsp hot sauce
1 Tbsp buttermilk
Tortilla wrappers

Instructions

1. Take a large bowl and mix together coleslaw mix, water, brown sugar, salt, apple cider vinegar, and red pepper flakes. Set aside.
2. Take another small bowl and combine mayonnaise, hot sauce, buttermilk, garlic powder, and salt. Set this mixture aside.
3. Select the Instant Pot Duo Crisp Air Fryer option, adjust the temperature to 360°F and push start. Preheating will start.
4. Create a clear station by placing two large flat pans side by side. Whisk together egg and buttermilk with salt and pepper in one of them. In the second, whisk flour, corn starch, black pepper, garlic powder, onion powder, salt, paprika, and cayenne pepper.
5. Cut the chicken tenders into 1-inch pieces. Season all pieces with a little salt and pepper.
6. Once the Instant Pot Duo Crisp Air Fryer is preheated, remove the tray and lightly spray it with oil. Coat your chicken with egg mixture while shaking off any excess egg, followed by the flour mixture, and place it on the tray and tray in the basket, making sure your chicken pieces don't overlap.
7. Close the Air Fryer lid, and cook on 360°F for 10 minutes, while flipping and spraying halfway through cooking.
8. Once the chicken is done, remove and place chicken into warmed tortilla shells. Top with coleslaw and spicy mayonnaise.

Nutrition Facts Per Serving

Calories 375, Total Fat 15g, Total Carbs 31g, Protein 29g

Chapter 5 Fish and Seafood

Coconut Shrimp

Prep time: 10 minutes, cook time: 15 minutes; Serves 2-4

10 Ingredients

1/2 cup flour
1 tsp kosher salt
3/4 cup plain breadcrumbs
1/2 cup shredded unsweetened coconut chopped
1/2 tsp white pepper
2 egg whites lightly beaten
1 pound Shrimp peeled and deveined
Sweet chili sauce or duck sauce
2 tsp lime zest
1 tsp salt

Instructions

1. Combine flour, salt, and white pepper in a dish. Add egg whites to a second dish. Combine breadcrumbs, coconut, lime zest, and salt in a third shallow dish.
2. Dredge the shrimp first in a flour mixture, then in the egg mixture, place the shrimp in the mixture of breadcrumb and press the crumbs firmly on all sides.
3. Divide the coated shrimp onto the cooking trays, leaving space between each piece.
4. Place the drip pan in the Instant Pot Duo Crisp Air Fryer basket. Using the display panel, select the option Air Fry, then adjust the temperature to 400°F and the time to 12 minutes.
5. Press start to begin preheating by closing the lid of Instant Pot Duo Crisp Air Fryer basket.
6. Turn the food over after 5 minutes and switch the cooking trays so that the one that was in the top-most position is now in the bottom-most position, and vice-versa.
7. When the program is complete, remove the shrimp and serve with your choice of dipping sauce.

Nutrition Facts Per Serving

Calories 406, Total Fat 9.2g, Total Carbs 48.4g, Protein 32.4g

Baked Shrimp Scampi

Prep time: 10 minutes, cook time: 10 minutes; Serves 4

9 Ingredients

1 lb large shrimp
8 tbsp butter
1 tbsp minced garlic (use 2 for extra garlic flavor)
1/4 cup white wine or cooking sherry
1/2 tsp salt
1/4 tsp cayenne pepper
1/4 tsp paprika
1/2 tsp onion powder
3/4 cup bread crumbs

Instructions

1. Take a bowl and mix the bread crumbs with dry seasonings.
2. On the stovetop (or in the Instant Pot on saute), melt the butter with the garlic and the white wine.
3. Remove from heat and add the shrimp and the bread crumb mix.
4. Transfer the mix to a casserole dish.
5. Choose the Bake operation and add food to the Instant Pot Duo Crisp Air Fryer. Close the lid and Bake at 350°F for 10 minutes or until they are browned.
6. Serve and enjoy.

Nutrition Facts Per Serving

Calories 422, Total Fat 26g, Total Carbs 18g, Protein 29 g

Air Fryer Marinated Salmon

Prep time: 5 minutes, cook time: 12 minutes; Serves 4

6 Ingredients

4 salmon fillets or 1 1lb fillet cut into 4 pieces
1 Tbsp brown sugar
½ Tbsp Minced Garlic
6 Tbsps Soy Sauce
¼ cup Dijon Mustard
1 Green onions finely chopped

Instructions

1. Take a bowl and whisk together soy sauce, dijon mustard, brown sugar, and minced garlic. Pour this mixture over salmon fillets, making sure that all the fillets are covered. Refrigerate and marinate for 20-30 minutes.
2. Remove salmon fillets from marinade and place them in greased or lined on the tray in the Instant Pot Duo Crisp Air Fryer basket, close the lid.
3. Select the Air Fry option and Air Fry for around 12 minutes at 400°F.
4. Remove from Instant Pot Duo Crisp Air Fryer and top with chopped green onions.

Nutrition Facts Per Serving

Calories 267, Total Fat 11g, Total Carbs 5g, Protein 37g

Coconut Shrimp with Dip

Prep time: 10 minutes, cook time: 9 minutes; Serves 4

8 Ingredients

1 lb large raw shrimp peeled and deveined with tail on
2 eggs beaten
¼ cup Panko Breadcrumbs
1 tsp salt
¼ tsp black pepper
½ cup All-Purpose Flour
½ cup unsweetened shredded coconut
Oil for spraying

Instructions

1. Clean and dry the shrimp. Set it aside.
2. Take 3 bowls. Put flour in the first bowl. Beat eggs in the second bowl. Mix coconut, breadcrumbs, salt, and black pepper in the third bowl.
3. Select the Air Fry option and adjust the temperature to 390°F. Push start and preheating will start.
4. Dip each shrimp in flour followed by the egg and then coconut mixture, ensuring shrimp is covered on all sides during each dip.
5. Once the preheating is done, place shrimp in a single layer on greased tray in the basket of the Instant Pot Duo Crisp Air Fryer.
6. Spray the shrimp with oil lightly, and then close the Air Fryer basket lid. Cook for around 4 minutes.
7. After 4 minutes, open the Air Fryer basket lid and flip the shrimp over. Respray the shrimp with oil, close the Air Fryer basket lid, and cook for five more minutes.
8. Remove shrimp from the basket and serve with Thai Sweet Chili Sauce.

Nutrition Facts Per Serving

Calories 279, Total Fat 11g, Total Carbs 17g, Protein 28g

Air Fryer Fish

Prep time: 10 minutes, cook time: 17 minutes; Serves 4

9 Ingredients

4-6 Whiting Fish fillets cut in half
Oil to mist

Fish Seasoning

¾ cup very fine cornmeal
¼ cup flour
2 tsp old bay
1 ½ tsp salt
1 tsp paprika
½ tsp garlic powder
½ tsp black pepper

Instructions

1. Put the ingredients for fish seasoning in a Ziplock bag and shake it well. Set aside.
2. Rinse and pat dry the fish fillets with paper towels. Make sure that they still are damp.
3. Place the fish fillets in a ziplock bag and shake until they are completely covered with seasoning.
4. Place the fillets on a baking rack to let any excess flour to fall off.
5. Grease the bottom of the Instant Pot Duo Crisp Air Fryer basket tray and place the fillets on the tray. Close the lid, select the Air Fry option and cook filets on 400°F for 10 minutes.
6. Open the Air Fryer lid and spray the fish with oil on the side facing up before flipping it over, ensure that the fish is fully coated. Flip and cook another side of the fish for 7 minutes. Remove the fish and serve.

Nutrition Facts Per Serving

Calories 193, Total Fat 1g, Total Carbs 27g, Protein 19g

Lobster Tails

Prep time: 5 minutes, cook time: 8 minutes; Serves 2

6 Ingredients

2 6oz lobster tails
1 tsp salt
1 tsp chopped chives
2 Tbsp unsalted butter melted
1 Tbsp minced garlic
1 tsp lemon juice

Instructions

1. Combine butter, garlic, salt, chives, and lemon juice to prepare butter mixture.
2. Butterfly lobster tails by cutting through shell followed by removing the meat and resting it on top of the shell.
3. Place them on the tray in the Instant Pot Duo Crisp Air Fryer basket and spread butter over the top of lobster meat. Close the Air Fryer lid, select the Air Fry option and cook on 380°F for 4 minutes.
4. Open the Air Fryer lid and spread more butter on top, cook for extra 2-4 minutes until done.

Nutrition Facts Per Serving

Calories 120, Total Fat 12g, Total Carbs 2g, Protein 1g

Chapter 6 Beef Lamb And Pork

Sweet & Sour Pork
Prep time: 12 minutes, cook time: 27 minutes; Serves 4
9 Ingredients
2 pounds Pork cut into chunks
2 large Eggs
1 teaspoon Pure Sesame Oil (optional)
1 cup Potato Starch (or cornstarch)
1/2 teaspoon Sea Salt
1/4 teaspoon Freshly Ground Black Pepper
1/16 teaspoon Chinese Five Spice
3 Tablespoons Canola Oil
Oil Mister
Instructions
1. In a mixing bowl, combine salt, potato starch, Chinese Five Spice, and peppers.
2. In another bowl, beat the eggs & add sesame oil.
3. Then dredge the pieces of Pork into the Potato Starch and remove the excess. Then dip each piece into the egg mixture, shake off excess, and then back into the Potato Starch mixture.
4. Place pork pieces into the Instant Pot Duo Crisp Air Fryer Basket after spray the pork with oil.
5. Close the Air Fryer lid and cook at 340°F for approximately 8 to12 minutes (or until pork is cooked), shaking the basket a couple of times for evenly distribution.
Nutrition Facts Per Serving
Calories 521, Total Fat 21g, Total Carbs 23g, Protein 60g

Air Fried Sausages

Prep time: 5 minutes, cook time: 13 minutes; Serves 6

2 Ingredients

6 sausage
olive oil spray

Instructions

1. Pour 1.5 cup of water into Instant Pot Duo Crisp Air Fryer. Place air fryer basket inside the pot, spray inside with nonstick spray and put sausage links inside.
2. Close the Air Fryer lid and steam for about 5 minutes.
3. Remove the lid once done. Spray links with olive oil and close air crisp lid.
4. Set to air crisp at 400°F for 8 min flipping halfway through so both sides get browned.

Nutrition Facts Per Serving

Calories 267, Total Fat 23g, Total Carbs 2g, Protein 13g

Crispy Breaded Pork Chop

Prep time: 3 minutes, cook time: 12 minutes; Serves 6

12 Ingredients

olive oil spray
6 3/4-inch thick center-cut boneless pork chops, fat trimmed (5 oz each)
kosher salt
1 large egg, beaten
1/2 cup panko crumbs, check labels for GF
1/3 cup crushed cornflakes crumbs
2 tbsp grated parmesan cheese
1 1/4 tsp sweet paprika
1/2 tsp garlic powder
1/2 tsp onion powder
1/4 tsp chili powder
1/8 tsp black pepper

Instructions

1. Preheat the Instant Pot Duo Crisp Air Fryer for 12 minutes at 400°F.
2. On both sides, season pork chops with half teaspoon kosher salt.
3. Then combine cornflake crumbs, panko, parmesan cheese, 3/4 tsp kosher salt, garlic powder, paprika, onion powder, chili powder, and black pepper in a large bowl.
4. Place the egg beat in another bowl. Dip the pork in the egg & then crumb mixture.
5. When the air fryer is ready, place 3 of the chops into the Instant Pot Duo Crisp Air Fryer Basket and spritz the top with oil.
6. Close the Air Fryer lid and cook for 12 minutes turning halfway, spritzing both sides with oil.
7. Set aside and repeat with the remaining.

Nutrition Facts Per Serving

Calories 281, Total Fat 13g, Total Carbs 8g, Protein 33g

Pigs In Blankets

Prep time: 3 minutes, cook time: 15 minutes; Serves 9

3 Ingredients
9 Back Bacon
3 Large Brazilian Sausages
Salt & Pepper

Instructions
1. Chop the sausages into three equal sizes so that they become mini sausages.
2. Now that you have nine equal-sized pieces of sausage, wrap them in the bacon so that each piece of sausage has one rasher of bacon.
3. Place them into the Instant Pot Duo Crisp Air Fryer Basket.
4. Close the Air Fryer lid and cook at 350°F for 15 minutes and then sprinkle with salt and pepper
5. Serve hot.

Nutrition Facts Per Serving
Calories 202, Total Fat 18g, Total Carbs 2g, Protein 8g

Pulled Pork Taquitos

Prep time: 10 minutes, cook time: 10 minutes; Serves 10

6 Ingredients

2 cup Shredded meat or filling of choice (pulled pork carnitas)
1/2 cup diced onion
1 cup shredded cheese of choice (pepper jack)
1 package flour or corn tortillas
Spray cooking oil (Avocado oil)
Salsa, sour cream, guacamole, and cheese for garnish

Instructions

1. Place the tortilla on a flat plate or a tray
2. Starting at one end of tortilla, add a small amount of meat, onion, and cheese on the tortilla and roll it.
3. Secure it with two toothpicks
4. Sprinkle all sides of the taquitos with cooking oil
5. Choose the Air Fry option on the appliance and set the temperature to 400°F. Push start and let the Instant Pot Duo Crisp Air Fryer preheat.
6. Place the taquitos on Air Fryer tray or in the Instant Pot Duo Crisp Air Fryer basket.
7. Repeat until Air Fryer trays or the basket are full. Do not crowd them. Close
8. Air fry for about 8 minutes until the taquitos are golden brown. Flip the taquitos halfway through. If using multiple trays, switch the trays at 6 minutes, flip the taquitos at 4 and switch the trays again at 2
9. Garnish with sour cream, guacamole, onion, and cheese.

Nutrition Facts Per Serving

Calories 190, Total Fat 10g, Total Carbs 13g, Protein 12g

Sausage and Onions

Prep time: 5 minutes, cook time: 30 minutes; Serves 4

4 Ingredients

20 ounces (or 2 packages) smoked sausage, sliced
2 onions, diced
2 Tbsp olive oil
Salt and Pepper to taste

Instructions

1. Place the onions into the Instant Pot Duo Crisp Air Fryer Basket.
2. Saute the onion in the Instant Pot, salt and pepper to taste, and saute until translucent.
3. Now add the sausage to the Instant Pot Duo Crisp Air Fryer Basket.
4. Close the Air Fryer lid and cook at 400°F for 25-30 minutes.

Nutrition Facts Per Serving

Calories 330, Total Fat 22g, Total Carbs 5g, Protein 28g

Roast Beef

Prep time: 5 minutes, cook time: 40 minutes; Serves 6

3 Ingredients

2.5-pound Beef Roast (can go up to 4 pounds)
1 Tablespoon Olive Oil
Seasoning to taste (Montreal Steak seasoning)

Instructions

1. Tie the roast to make it fit in the Instant Pot Duo Crisp Air Fryer.
2. Rub the roast with some olive oil.
3. Add the seasoning as per your preference.
4. Place the roast in the Air Fryer basket.
5. Close the lid and select the Air fry option. Air Fry the beef at 360°F for approximately 15 minutes per pound for medium-rare beef.
6. Let the roast rest for around 5 minutes and serve.

Nutrition Facts Per Serving

Calories 433, Total Fat 29g, Total Carbs 0g, Protein 43g

Pork Tenderloin

Prep time: 10 minutes, cook time: 28 minutes; Serves 4

8 Ingredients

1 lb pork tenderloin
Cooking oil spray of choice
1 tbsp grain mustard
1 tbsp dijon mustard
2 tbsp honey (or substitute Vita Fiber for Keto option)
2 tbsp soy sauce
1 tbsp minced garlic
1 tsp sriracha sauce (adjust to taste)

Instructions

1. Combine the soy sauce, mustard, honey (or Vita Fiber), garlic, and sriracha and put that into a large baggie
2. Add the pork tenderloin and marinate for a few minutes to up to 24 hours
3. Choose the Air Fry option from the Instant Pot Duo Crisp Air Fryer. Set the temperature to 380°F and push start to begin preheating.
4. Sprinkle the Air Fryer tray with cooking oil and place the tenderloin on the tray and brush it with extra sauce. Close the lid of the appliance after putting the tray in it.
5. Air fry for about 26 minutes, turning the tenderloin after every 4-5 minutes and brushing it with sauce each time. The roast will get dark brown.
6. The pork is properly done when a thermometer inserted lengthwise into the thickest part of the meat registers at least 145°F. Cook to 165°F for well done.
7. Let the pork rest while covered in foil for about 5-10 minutes
8. Slice and serve the dish.

Nutrition Facts Per Serving

Calories 319, Total Fat 11g, Total Carbs 14g, Protein 41g

Jamaican Jerk Pork

Prep time: 10 minutes, cook time: 20 minutes; Serves 4

3 Ingredients

1.5 lbs pork butt chopped into large 3-inch pieces
¼ cup jerk paste
oil for spraying basket

Instructions

1. Rub the pork pieces with jerk paste and allow it to marinate the pork for 4 to 24 hours in the refrigerator. The longer, the better.
2. Choose the Air Fry option and adjust the temperature to 390°F. Push start and the Instant Pot Duo Crisp Air Fryer will begin preheating.
3. Spray the bottom of the Air Fryer basket.
4. Remove the pork from the refrigerator and allow to rest at room temp for 20 minutes. Once preheating is completed, place the pork in Instant Pot Duo Crisp Air Fryer ensuring the pieces are spaced apart. Set the timer for 20 minutes, and cook while flipping halfway.
5. Remove from the air fryer and allow it to sit for 5-10 minutes before cutting.

Nutrition Facts Per Serving

Calories 205, Total Fat 9g, Total Carbs 0g, Protein 31g

Juicy Air Fryer Steak

Prep time: 20 minutes, cook time: 12 minutes; Serves 2

9 Ingredients

2 8 oz Ribeye steak
salt
freshly cracked black pepper
olive oil

Garlic Butter

1 stick unsalted butter softened
2 Tbsp fresh parsley chopped
2 tsp garlic minced
1 tsp Worcestershire Sauce
1/2 tsp salt

Instructions

1. Mix butter, parsley garlic, Worcestershire sauce, and salt until thoroughly combined to make Garlic Butter.
2. Place in parchment paper and roll into a log. Refrigerate until ready to use.
3. Remove steak from the fridge and allow to sit at room temperature for 20 minutes. Rub a little bit of olive oil on both sides of the steak and season with salt and freshly cracked black pepper.
4. Grease your Instant Pot Duo Crisp Air Fryer basket by rubbing a little bit of oil on the basket. Choose the Air Fry option and set the temperature to 400°F, push start. Once preheated, place the steaks in the Instant Pot Duo Crisp Air Fryer and cook for 12 minutes, flipping halfway through. Cook for 10 minutes for medium-rare steak and 14 minutes for medium-well steak.
5. Remove from Instant Pot Duo Crisp Air Fryer and allow it to rest for 5 minutes. Top with garlic butter.

Nutrition Facts Per Serving

Calories 674, Total Fat 74g, Total Carbs 0g, Protein 2g

Perfect Air Fryer Pork Chops

Prep time: 15 minutes, cook time: 15 minutes; Serves 4

9 Ingredients

4 thick-cut pork chops
1/2 tsp black pepper
2 tsp oregano
1 tsp rosemary
1 tsp paprika
2 tsp sage
2 tsp thyme1 tsp garlic powder
1 tsp salt

Instructions

1. Mix the sage, oregano, rosemary, paprika, thyme, garlic powder, salt, and black pepper. Set this mixture aside.
2. Choose the Air Fry option and set the temperature of the Instant Pot Duo Crisp Air Fryer to 360°F. Push start to begin preheating.
3. While the Air Fryer is preheating, rub olive oil over the pork chops and sprinkle the herb mixture over the chops while covering all sides.
4. Once it is preheated, place the pork chops on the tray of the Air Fryer basket and make sure that the chops don't overlap.
5. Close the lid and cook on 360°F for 14 to 16 minutes while flipping halfway (for flipping, you need to lift the lid, it will automatically stop cooking), Pork chops are done when they have reached an internal temperature of 145°F.
6. Remove the pork chops from Instant Pot Duo Crisp Air Fryer and cover them with foil. Allow them to rest for 5 minutes.

Nutrition Facts Per Serving

Calories 214, Total Fat 10g, Total Carbs 2g, Protein 29g

Chapter 7 Snacks And Appetizers

Air Fried Turkey and Fajitas

Prep time: 5 minutes, cook time: 20 minutes; Serves 2

13 Ingredients
6 Tortilla Wraps
3.5oz Leftover Turkey Breast
1 Large Avocado
1 Large Yellow Pepper
1 Large Red Pepper
1 Large Green Pepper
½ Small Red Onion
5 Tbsp Soft Cheese
3 Tbsp Cajun Spice
2 Tbsp Mexican Seasoning
1 Tsp Cumin
Salt & Pepper
0.35oz Fresh Coriander

Instructions
1. Slice up the salad and chop the avocado into little wedges.
2. Chop up the turkey breast into small little chunks.
3. Place the turkey, peppers, and onions into a bowl and mix with all the seasonings along with the soft cheese.
4. Then dice the red onion. Slice the peppers into thin slices.
5. Place them into the Instant Pot Duo Crisp Air Fryer Tray.
6. Close the Air Fryer lid and cook for 20 minutes on 390°F.
7. Serve when ready.

Nutrition Facts Per Serving
Calories 711, Total Fat 39g, Total Carbs 60g, Protein 30g

Five Cheese Pull-Apart Bread

Prep time: 15 minutes, cook time: 4 minutes; Serves 2

10 Ingredients
1 Large Bread Loaf
3.5oz Butter
2 Tsp Garlic Puree
1oz Cheddar Cheese
1oz Goats Cheese
1oz Mozzarella Cheese
1oz Soft Cheese
1oz Edam Cheese
2 Tsp Chives
Salt & Pepper

Instructions
1. Grate the hard cheese into four different piles and put it to one side.
2. In a saucepan melt the butter on moderate heat. Add garlic, chives, salt, and pepper. Cook for a further two minutes and mix well. Put it to one side.
3. Using a good quality bread knife creates little slits into the bread. In each of the slit, wholes cover with garlic butter until you have done all of them. Then cover them with soft cheese in order to give them a creamy taste.
4. In every alternative one, place a little goats' cheese and a little cheddar.
5. Then the ones that have not been filled, add the Edam and mozzarella.
6. Place them into the Instant Pot Duo Crisp Air Fryer Basket.
7. Close the Air Fryer lid and cook for 4 minutes at 290°F.
8. Serve Hot.

Nutrition Facts Per Serving
Calories 640, Total Fat 60g, Total Carbs 9g, Protein 16g

Zucchini Fritters

Prep time: 5 minutes, cook time: 6 minutes; Serves 4

8 Ingredients
3.5oz Plain Flour
1 Medium Egg beat
5 Tbsp Milk
5.29oz Grated Courgette
2.6oz Spring Onion thinly sliced
0.9oz Cheddar Cheese grated
1 Tbsp Mixed Herbs
Salt & Pepper

Instructions
1. Preheat the Instant Pot Duo Crisp Air Fryer at 360°F.
2. Grate the zucchini and make sure to remove any excessive moisture.
3. Put the plain flour into a bowl and add the seasoning.
4. Whisk the egg and milk and then add to the flour to make a smooth creamy batter.
5. Stir in the cheese.
6. Add in the zucchini and the spring onion. Mix it well.
7. If the batter isn't very thick then add more flour and cheese to it until it is of a reasonable thick pancake-like mixture.
8. Make them into small burger shapes and place them into the Instant Pot Duo Crisp Air Fryer Basket.
9. Close the Air Fryer lid and cook at 360°F temperature for 6 minutes.
10. Serve it with mayonnaise.

Nutrition Facts Per Serving
Calories 165, Total Fat 5g, Total Carbs 23g, Protein 7g

Air Fried Croutons

Prep time: 3 minutes, cook time: 8 minutes; Serves 9
2 Ingredients
2 Slices Wholemeal Bread
1 Tbsp Olive Oil
Instructions
11. Chop the slices of bread into med chunks.
12. Place them into the Instant Pot Duo Crisp Air Fryer Basket.
13. Add the olive oil.
14. Close the Air Fryer lid and cook for eight minutes at 390°F.
15. Serve over the soup or as a snack.
Nutrition Facts Per Serving
Calories 23, Total Fat 1g, Total Carbs 3g, Protein 0.5g

Mini Empanadas with Chorizo

Prep time: 20 minutes, cook time: 20 minutes; Serves 2

5 Ingredients
1 shallot, finely chopped
¼ red bell pepper, diced into small cubes
7.05oz chilled pie crust dough (pâte brisée) or pizza dough
4.4oz chorizo, in small cubes
2 tablespoons parsley

Instructions
1. Stir the chorizo with the bell pepper and shallot in a skillet and fry on a low heat for 3 to 4 minutes. Fry until the bell pepper is tender. Remove the heat and stir in the parsley. Allow the mixture to cool.
2. Preheat the Instant Pot Duo Crisp Air Fryer at 390°F.
3. Use a glass to cut twenty rounds from the dough, each 5 cm in size. Scoop a full spoon of the chorizo mixture onto each round. Then press the edges together between the index finger and the thumb, making a scallop pattern.
4. Put ten empanadas into the Instant Pot Duo Crisp Air Fryer Basket.
5. Close the Air Fryer lid and bake the empanadas for 10 minutes.
6. Using the same steps bake the remaining empanadas. Serve the empanadas lukewarm.

Nutrition Facts Per Serving
Calories 204, Total Fat 13.6g, Total Carbs 5g, Protein 15.3g

Onion Rings

Prep time: 10 minutes, cook time: 6 minutes; Serves 4

9 Ingredients
1 Large Onion
2 Bread Maker Gluten Free Rolls
2 Large Eggs
4.23oz Oat Flour
1 Tbsp Basil
1 Tsp Garlic Puree
1 Tsp Paprika
½ Tsp Mustard Powder
Salt & Pepper

Instructions
1. Place eggs and garlic into a bowl and using a fork beat the eggs.
2. Place them into a second bowl and mix oat flour along with salt, pepper, and mustard.
3. Blend your gluten-free bread rolls and place them into a third bowl along with the rest of the seasonings.
4. Make sure each bowl is well mixed with its seasonings.
5. Slice your onion into rings.
6. Place each of your onion rings into the oat flour bowl, the egg bowl, and the breadcrumbs bowl until it is well mixed.
7. Shake off any excess batter
8. Place the onion rings into the Instant Pot Duo Crisp Air Fryer Basket.
9. Close the Air Fryer lid and select the Air Fry option and cook for 6 minutes at 400°F and serve with your favorite dipping sauce.

Nutrition Facts Per Serving
Calories 263, Total Fat 7g, Total Carbs 41g, Protein 9g

Pizza Pasta

Prep time: 5 minutes, cook time: 25 minutes; Serves 8

9 Ingredients

1/2 lb to 1 lb Italian sausage
6 oz pepperoni (sliced)
1 medium onion
2 Tbsp minced garlic
1/2 tsp oregano
1/2 tsp basil
1/4 tsp ground black pepper
1/2 tsp salt
1/4 tsp crushed red pepper
2 cup chicken stock
1 cup red wine (or substitute chicken stock)
1 28 oz can dice Italian tomatoes, whit juice
1 28 oz can tomato puree
16 oz pasta (I used rigatoni)
8 oz shredded Italian or Mozzarella cheese

Instructions

1. Mix Italian sausage, onion, and garlic in Instant Pot Duo Crisp Air Fryer basket.
2. Add the spices and stir well.
3. Add half of the pepperoni, the chicken stock, and red wine.
4. Add the tomatoes and tomatoes puree. Stir lightly.
5. Pour the pasta on top of the liquid and gently press down until the pasta is covered with liquid. Do not stir. The idea is to keep most of the pasta off of the bottom of the pot.
6. Select the option Air Fryer. Close the Air Fryer lid and cook for 6 minutes.
7. Stir in 1/3 of the cheese and place the rest on top of the pasta mix.
8. Layer the remaining pepperoni on top of the cheese.
9. Close the Air Fryer lid and cook at 400°F for 5 minutes.
10. Remove the air fryer lid and serve!

Nutrition Facts Per Serving

Calories 581, Total Fat 33g, Total Carbs 42g, Protein 29g

Air Fried French Fries

Prep time: 5 minutes, cook time: 13 minutes; Serves 6

5 Ingredients

2 Potatoes Russett, medium or large in size
3/4 tbsp Olive Oil
1/2 tsp Salt
1/4 tsp Black Pepper
1/2 tsp Garlic powder

Instructions

1. Arrange the seasoned potato slices and place them at the bottom of your air fryer basket.
2. Potatoes will be crispier if they'll be separated.
3. Close the Air Fryer lid
4. Select the option Air Fryer and cook fries at 360ºF for 20 minutes.
5. Toss the fries halfway through. If you want fries to be more crisper, allow to cook for 2 more additional minutes.
6. Serve hot.

Nutrition Facts Per Serving

Calories 95, Total Fat 3g, Total Carbs 14g, Protein 3g

Air Fryer Crispy Tofu Buffalo Bites

Prep time: 10 minutes, cook time: 15 minutes; Serves 6

9 Ingredients

13oz Extra-firm Tofu
1/2 cup Franks Hot sauce
1/2 cup Chickpea flour
1/2 tsp Garlic powder
salt to taste
1 1/2 cup Panko breadcrumbs (Gluten-free version)
1/4 cup Rice flour
Few Tbsp water to make a thick batter
oil spray

Instructions

1. Press the tofu for thirty minutes. (Drain tofu and then wrap in paper towels or clean tea towel, and place heavy items on top to press.
2. Combine in a bowl chickpea flour, garlic powder, and salt.
3. Add in a little water to make the batter thick.
4. Cut the tofu into the sticks or nugget sized pieces.
5. Coat tofu with rice flour then in the chickpea flour batter
6. Coat it with the panko breadcrumbs.
7. Place the tofu into the Instant Pot Duo Crisp Air Fryer Basket. Spray oil on the tofu.
8. Select the option Air Fryer.
9. Close the Air Fryer lid and cook at 400°F for a total of 15 minutes. Turn them after seven minutes until browned and crispy. Repeat with remaining tofu.
10. Put the Air-fryer tofu in a large mixing bowl and toss with the buffalo sauce to coat. Serve immediately with celery and ranch sauce.

Nutrition Facts Per Serving

Calories 387, Total Fat 23g, Total Carbs 4g, Protein 41g

Curried Sweet Potato Fries With Creamy Cumin Ketchup

Prep time: 10 minutes, cook time: 60 minutes; Serves 2

10 Ingredients
For the Sweet Potato Fries
2 small sweet potatoes
2-3 tablespoons olive oil
1/2 teaspoon curry powder
1/4 teaspoon coriander
1/4 teaspoon sea salt
For the Creamy Cumin Ketchup
1/4 cup ketchup
2 tablespoons vegan mayo - A less tangy one works best here.
1/2 teaspoon ground cumin
1/8 teaspoon ground ginger
pinch of cinnamon

Instructions

1. Cut the sweet potatoes into about 1/4 sticks. They should be as wide around as your pinky finger, but longer is also fine.
2. Arrange the sweet potato sticks on a cookie sheet, and spray 2 tablespoons of the olive oil over them. Also, sprinkle on the coriander, curry powder, and sea salt. Toss them well to coat them properly in the oil, spices, and salt. Add the rest of the oil, if required.
3. Air Fryer usage directions: No preheating required. Transfer the sweet potato fries to the Instant Pot Duo Crisp Air Fryer basket. Choose the Air Fry option and close the lid. Cook at 370°F for about 20 minutes, shaking them after 10 minutes.
4. For Making the Creamy Cumin Ketchup, whisk all of the ingredients together in a small bowl.

Nutrition Facts Per Serving
Calories 189, Total Fat 17g, Total Carbs 9g, Protein 0g

Fried Hot Dogs

Prep time: 3 minutes, cook time: 7 minutes; Serves 2

3 Ingredients

2 hot dogs
2 hot dog buns
2 tablespoons grated cheese

Instructions

1. Preheat Instant Pot Duo Crisp Air Fryer to 390°F.
2. Place two hot dogs into the air fryer basket.
3. Close the Air Fryer lid and cook for about 5 minutes.
4. Remove the hot dog from the air fryer.
5. Place the hot dog on a bun, add cheese if desired.
6. Place dressed hot dog into the Instant Pot Duo Crisp Air Fryer, and cook for an additional 2 minutes.

Nutrition Facts Per Serving

Calories 843, Total Fat 13g, Total Carbs 29g, Protein 12g

Sweet Potato Chips

Prep time: 10 minutes, cook time: 50 minutes; Serves 2

4 Ingredients

2 medium-sized Sweet Potatoes thinly sliced
¼ cup of Olive Oil
1 teaspoon of ground Cinnamon optional
Salt and Pepper to taste

Instructions

1. Thinly slice the sweet potatoes. Use a mandolin or a food processor.
2. Soak the sweet potato slices in the cold water for thirty minutes.
3. Drain and pat dry the slices thoroughly. Repeat it multiple times till completely dry. This is an important step to ensure crispy chips.
4. Toss the sweet potato slices with salt, olive oil, pepper, and cinnamon (if using), ensuring every slice is coated with the oil.
5. Place the slices into the Instant Pot Duo Crisp Air Fryer Basket.
6. Press the start button to air fry the sweet potatoes at 390°F for twenty minutes, giving the basket a shake every seven to eight minutes for even cooking. If it is still not crisp, air fry for an additional 5 minutes.
7. Serve it hot with ketchup.

Nutrition Facts Per Serving

Calories 327, Total Fat 25.2g, Total Carbs 23g, Protein 2g

Parmesan Truffle Fries

Prep time: 10 minutes, cook time: 15 minutes; Serves 2

7 Ingredients

2 large gold potatoes, peeled
1 tablespoon parsley flakes
1/2 teaspoon garlic powder
1 teaspoon black pepper, crushed
1/2 teaspoon truffle salt
olive oil spray
2 tablespoons parmesan cheese

Instructions

1. Use a mandoline with a French fry setting, slice the whole potato using the spring-form handle to slice into French fries.
2. Place sliced potatoes in a bowl and spray with olive spray for about 3 seconds. Add garlic powder, black pepper, and parsley flakes.
3. Place all of them into the Instant Pot Duo Crisp Air Fryer Basket.
4. Close the Air Fryer lid and cook for about 5 minutes at 390°F.
5. Take out the basket and flip fries in order to evenly cook the fries. Cook another 8 minutes and remove from the Air Fryer and add to a bowl. Sprinkle with truffle salt and parmesan cheese.

Nutrition Facts Per Serving

Calories 188, Total Fat 10g, Total Carbs 14.3g, Protein 10.3g

Chicken Nuggets

Prep time: 4 minutes, cook time: 16 minutes; Serves 4

7 Ingredients

16 oz 2 large skinless boneless chicken breasts, cut into even 1-inch bite-sized pieces
1/2 teaspoon kosher salt and black pepper, to taste
2 teaspoons olive oil
6 tablespoons whole wheat Italian seasoned breadcrumbs
2 tablespoons panko
2 tablespoons grated parmesan cheese
olive oil spray

Instructions

1. Preheat the Instant Pot Duo Crisp Air Fryer at 400°F for eight minutes.
2. Put olive oil in one bowl and the panko, breadcrumbs, and parmesan cheese in another.
3. Season the chicken using salt and pepper, then put it in the bowl with the olive oil and mix it well so the olive oil evenly coats all of the chicken.
4. Put a few chunks of chicken one at a time into the breadcrumb mixture to coat.
5. Place them into the Instant Pot Duo Crisp Air Fryer Basket.
6. Then lightly spray the top of it with olive oil spray.
7. Close the Air Fryer lid and cook for 8 minutes, turning halfway until it gets golden.

Nutrition Facts Per Serving

Calories 173, Total Fat 4.5g, Total Carbs 8g, Protein 25g

Mini Popovers

Prep time: 5 minutes, cook time: 20 minutes; Serves 4-7

5 Ingredients

1 cup milk room temperature
2 eggs room temperature
1 tbsp butter melted
1 cup all-purpose flour
Salt and pepper Pinch of each

Instructions

1. Generously coat a heatproof silicone egg bite mold with nonstick spray.
2. Add all ingredients to a blender and process at medium speed for 30 seconds.
3. Fill each mold with a scant 2 tbsp of batter.
4. Place them into the Instant Pot Duo Crisp Air Fryer Basket.
5. Select the option Air Fryer, Close the Air Fryer lid and cook at 400°F for 20 minutes.
6. After twenty minutes place the egg bite mold on the lower tray of the Instant Pot Duo Crisp Air Fryer.
7. After it gets cooked quickly pierce each popover with a sharp knife, then again place them in the Instant Pot Duo Crisp Air Fryer Basket and continue cooking for 1-2 minutes more.
8. Serve immediately.

Nutrition Facts Per Serving

Calories 135, Total Fat 4.6g, Total Carbs 17.9g, Protein 5.6g

Air Fryer Risotto Balls

Prep time: 20 minutes, cook time: 10 minutes; Serves 4

7 Ingredients

Risotto
1 T olive oil
1 cup onions diced very small
4 cups vegetable broth
1 cup arborio rice
1 cup parmesan cheese

Breading
1.5 cups Bread Crumbs I used Ian's GF Italian Pankos
2 eggs beaten

Instructions
1. If using the leftover risotto, go to step 6.
2. Add some olive oil to a deep and large saucepan and heat it over over medium heat. Post this, add the onions and saute until soft.
3. Add dry rice to the pan and saute for around 1 minute.
4. After this, add 2 cups of veggie broth. Let the broth cook down while continually stir to avoid any burning. Once the liquid has been cooked properly, add 2 more cups of veggie broth. Continue with this process until all the liquid is absorbed and your rice is soft. This process should take around 20 minutes. Stir in parmesan.
5. Put risotto into a casserole dish or sheet pan. Cool for around 1-2 hours in the fridge. (The risotto has to be properly cooled to be able to be rolled into balls).
6. Take a small bowl and place the bread crumbs. In another container, store the beaten eggs.
7. Remove the chilled risotto (rice mixture) from the fridge. Roll into 1-inch rice balls. Dip them into eggs then into bread crumbs to coat the entire ball. Do this until you run out of ingredients.
8. Place rolled and coated balls back into the fridge for 45 minutes.
9. Remove from the fridge and place it on the trays of the Instant Pot Duo Crisp Air Fryer in small batches. Choose the Air Fry option on the appliance and close the lid.
10. Air Fry at 400°F for a cooking time of 10 minutes. Shake for 8 minutes. The balls are properly done around minute 6-7 but the browning doesn't happen until minute 8-10.
11. Serve with marinara sauce.

Nutrition Facts Per Serving
Calories 255, Total Fat 7g, Total Carbs 38g, Protein 10g

Chicken Tenders

Prep time: 5 minutes, cook time: 16 minutes; Serves 12

9 Ingredients

1 pound skinless, chicken tenders or chicken breast cut into strips
1/2 cup grated Parmesan cheese
1/2 cup Panko breadcrumbs or other breadcrumbs of choice
2 eggs
1/3 cup all-purpose flour
1/2 cup milk or Buttermilk (preferred)
1 teaspoon Italian Seasoning
Salt and pepper to taste
Cooking oil spray (avocado oil)

Instructions

1. Choose the Air Fry option on the Instant Pot Duo Crisp Air Fryer and set the temperature to 400°F. Push start and begin the preheating.
2. Put the chicken tenders in a bag with a ziplock or bowl and coat them with milk
3. Combine the breadcrumbs, salt and pepper, seasoning and Parmesan cheese in a deep bowl.
4. Place the egg in the other bowl and flour in a separate bowl.
5. Dig the tenders through the flour followed by dipping in egg, post dredge through the breadcrumb mix.
6. Once preheated, sprinkle the Air Fryer trays or basket with oil and place the tenders on the tray. Do not crowd or overlap the tenders.
7. Drizzle the chicken tenders with some oil.
8. Close the Air fryer lid and Air Fry for about 5 minutes, then turn the tenders over and spray them with oil again. Switch the tray positions in case you are using multiple trays.
9. Repeat step 8 again.
10. Air fry for another 6 minutes or until the chicken tenders are golden brown and internal temperature is at least 165°F, flipping the tenders or switching trays as necessary.

Nutrition Facts Per Serving

Calories 359, Total Fat 15g, Total Carbs 19g, Protein 37g

Chicken Empanadas

Prep time: 10 minutes, cook time: 10 minutes; Serves 6

8 Ingredients

2 pounds shredded chicken
Package of chicken taco seasoning (or another seasoning mix of choice, Frontera Chicken skillet)
1/2 onion diced
1 cup shredded cheese of choice (cheddar)
2 frozen pie crusts, thawed
A dusting of flour (to roll out the crust)
Spray cooking oil of choice (coconut or avocado oil)
garnishes (sour cream, salsa, guacamole)

Instructions

1. Push the Air Fry button on the Instant Pot Duo Crisp Air Fryer. Set the prescribed temperature and push start to begin preheating.
2. Shred the meat properly
3. Take a medium bowl and mix the meat along with onion, sauce, and cheese
4. Roll out to each pie crust over the dusting of flour
5. Using a ramekin or small bowl to make a circle imprint on the dough
6. Cut out the circle finely
7. Cut additional circles by re-rolling the dough
8. Add a small amount of filling on each circle and fold over to form a half-circle shape
9. Pinch or crimp the dough and shut using a fork
10. Once the appliance is preheated, add food to the Air Fry tray and Close the lid. Air fry for around 10 minutes, turning the empanadas half way though
11. Garnish with salsa and sour cream and/or guacamole

Nutrition Facts Per Serving

Calories 456, Total Fat 20g, Total Carbs 22g, Protein 47g

Mozzarella Balls

Prep time: 80 minutes, cook time: 10 minutes; Serves 12

8 Ingredients

2 cups fresh grated mozzarella
3 tbsp cornstarch
1 egg
1 cup Italian seasoned breadcrumbs
1 tbsp oregano
1 1/2 tsp garlic powder
1 tsp salt
1 1/2 tbsp Parmesan

Instructions

1. Choose the Air Fry option and set the temperature of the Instant Pot Duo Crisp Air Fryer to 400°F.
2. Line a baking sheet with the parchment.
3. Make a thorough mixture of cornstarch and Parmesan to shredded cheese.
4. Roll the cheese into the bite-size balls and put it in the freezer (45- 60 mins).
5. Beat your egg in a small bowl.
6. Combine salt, garlic powder, and bread crumbs and mix well in another bowl.
7. Immerse your cheese balls in the egg and coat them well.
8. Roll the egg coated balls in bread crumbs and place them back on a baking sheet.
9. Put this in the freezer for around 20 mins.
10. Repeat the egg and bread steps and place it in the Air Fryer basket. Close the lid.
11. Cook on 400°F for around 10 minutes while making sure to rotate frequently.
12. When the balls begin to melt, transfer them back to your baking sheet. Let rest for a couple of minutes.

Nutrition Facts Per Serving

Calories 198, Total Fat 14g, Total Carbs 5g, Protein 13g

Swedish Meatballs

Prep time: 15 minutes, cook time: 25 minutes; Serves 4-6

10 Ingredients

2 slices white bread
1/2 cup milk
8 ounces ground beef
8 ounces ground pork
1/4 yellow onion, grated
3/4 teaspoon ground allspice
1 large egg
Kosher salt and freshly ground black pepper
Nonstick cooking spray, for the tray
Lingonberry jam, for serving

Instructions

1. Soak the bread in milk in a medium bowl for around 5 minutes. Squeeze out excess milk and tear into bite-sized pieces. Mix the bread with the ground beef, 1 teaspoon salt, pork, onion, allspice, egg, and a few grinds of pepper. Form this into small balls about the size of a heaping tablespoon.
2. Spray the basket of the Instant Pot Duo Crisp Air Fryer with cooking spray and fill it with the meatballs. Set the Instant Pot Duo Crisp Air Fryer to 360°F and close the lid. Cook while shaking the tray halfway through, until they are browned, tender and cooked through for about 10 minutes. Serve them with lingonberry jam.

Nutrition Facts Per Serving

Calories 153, Total Fat 5g, Total Carbs 4g, Protein 23g

Stuffed Mushrooms

Prep time: 15 minutes, cook time: 30 minutes; Serves 4-6

9 Ingredients

1/4 cup breadcrumbs
1/4 cup grated Pecorino-Romano
1 teaspoon chopped fresh mint
1 clove garlic, minced
4 tablespoons olive oil
1 tablespoon chopped fresh parsley
36 white button mushrooms (about 1 1/2 pounds), stemmed
Kosher salt and freshly ground black pepper
2 tablespoons shredded mozzarella

Instructions

1. In a medium bowl, combine the mozzarella, parsley, mint, garlic, 2 tablespoons of olive oil, breadcrumbs, Pecorino-Romano, 1/2 teaspoon salt, and 1/4 teaspoon pepper, and toss to blend.
2. In a large bowl, toss the mushrooms with the remaining 2 tablespoons of olive oil and arrange on a small baking sheet or plate with the cavities facing up.
3. Divide the breadcrumb mixture among the mushrooms while filling the cavities and pressing down gently to secure.
4. Place half the mushrooms in a single layer in the basket of the Instant Pot Duo Crisp Air Fryer. Set the Air Fryer to 360°F and close the lid. Cook until the filling is bubbling and browned about 10 minutes. Repeat with the remaining mushrooms.

Nutrition Facts Per Serving

Calories 181, Total Fat 13g, Total Carbs 8g, Protein 8g

Mexican Street Style Corn on the Cob

Prep time: 5 minutes, cook time: 15 minutes; Serves 4

7 Ingredients
4 ears shucked corn
½ cup Mexican Crema or Sour Cream
¼ cup Cotija Cheese grated
2 Tbsp cilantro finely chopped
2 tsp chili powder
Juice of 1 lime
Oil for spraying Vegetable, Canola, or Avocado

Instructions
1. Wash and dry the corn. Place the corn on the tray in the Instant Pot Duo Crisp Air Fryer basket in a single layer and lightly spray it with oil.
2. Choose the Air Fry option. Set the Air Fryer temperature to 400°F and timer for 15 minutes. Begin Air frying.
3. After exactly 8 minutes, open the lid, and turn corn and lightly spray again. Continue cooking.
4. Once the time is up, remove corn to a platter.
5. Spread Mexican crema on sides of the corn. Sprinkle with cotija cheese, chili powder, and cilantro. Squeeze with lime before serving.

Nutrition Facts Per Serving
Calories 177, Total Fat 9g, Total Carbs 19g, Protein 5g

Sweet and Spicy Bacon Wrapped Chicken

Prep time: 10 minutes, cook time: 13 minutes; Serves 4

5 Ingredients

1 lb chicken breast cut into 1-inch pieces
6 slices bacon cut into thirds*
1/3 cup brown sugar
1/2 Tbsp chili powder
1/8 tsp cayenne pepper

Instructions

1. Place one piece of chicken on one end of a piece of bacon. Secure each one with a toothpick after rolling it up.
2. Combine chili powder, brown sugar, and cayenne pepper in a bowl and stir. Use this mixture to coat each bacon-wrapped chicken piece.
3. Place bacon-wrapped chicken pieces on the tray in the Instant Pot Duo Crisp Air Fryer Basket, make sure that they have enough space between them. Close the lid, choose the Air Fry option and cook at 390°F for 13-15 minutes.

Nutrition Facts Per Serving

Calories 328, Total Fat 16g, Total Carbs 18g, Protein 28g

Avocado Egg Rolls

Prep time: 10 minutes, cook time: 10 minutes; Serves 4

16 Ingredients

Avocado Egg Rolls

3 avocados halved, pit removed, cubed and copped out
1 Roma tomato
1/4 cup red onion
2 Tbsp cilantro chopped
1 garlic clove minced
2 Tbsp fresh lime juice
8 egg roll wrappers
1 large egg beaten
salt and pepper

Cilantro Honey Dipping Sauce

1/2 cup cilantro chopped
1/4 cup honey
1 1/2 Tbsp apple cider vinegar
1 garlic clove minced
1/2 Tbsp olive oil
1 tsp fresh lime juice
salt and pepper

Instructions

1. Mix the Ingredients for Cilantro Honey Dipping Sauce and set the mixture aside.
2. Prepare the Avocado Egg Roll by placing avocado, garlic clove, Roma tomato, red onion, cilantro, and fresh lime juice in a large bowl. Combine them gently. Salt and pepper to taste.
3. Use the beaten egg and rub it around the edges of the egg roll wrapper. Place 1/3 cup of the avocado mixture in each egg roll wrapper and roll, thus sealing the edge.
4. Use a brush and spread the remaining egg wash on top of egg rolls.
5. Choose the Air Fry option and set the temperature of the Instant Pot Duo Crisp Air Fryer to 400°F. Push start for preheating.
6. Once preheating is done, spray oil inside of the Instant Pot Duo Crisp Air Fryer basket. Place the rolls in the air fryer and cook them for around 10 minutes while flipping them halfway.
7. Remove and allow them to cool. Egg rolls are done when wrappers are golden.
8. Serve egg rolls with Cilantro Honey Dipping Sauce.

Nutrition Facts Per Serving

Calories 441, Total Fat 25g, Total Carbs 47g, Protein 7g

Sweet and Spicy Brussel Sprouts

Prep time: 5 minutes, cook time: 20 minutes; Serves 4

5 Ingredients

1 lb brussels sprouts cut in half
2 tbsp honey
1 1/2 tbsp vegetable oil
1 tbsp gochujang
1/2 tsp salt

Instructions

1. Mix honey, vegetable oil, gochujang, and salt in a bowl and stir thoroughly. Set aside 1 Tbsp of the sauce. Add the Brussels sprouts to a bowl and stir them until all sprouts are fully covered.
2. Place your brussels sprouts in the Instant Pot Duo Crisp Air Fryer, ensuring that they are not overlapping with each other. Close the Air Fryer lid and choose the Air Fry option. Cook at 360°F for 15 minutes, shaking the basket halfway through or stir the ingredients for the uniform coooking.
3. Once 15 minutes timer is up, increase the temperature to 390°F and cook for five more minutes. When sprouts are done, place in a bowl and cover with reserved sauce and stir.

Nutrition Facts Per Serving

Calories 137, Total Fat 5g, Total Carbs 20g, Protein 3g

Crispy Air Fried Chicken Wings

Prep time: 10 minutes, cook time: 30 minutes; Serves 4

12 Ingredients

2 lbs chicken wings
¾ cup corn starch
1 tsp garlic powder
1 tsp onion powder
½ tsp salt

Korean Air Fried Chicken Sauce

2 Tbsp gochujang Korean chili paste
3 Tbsp honey
2 Tbsp brown sugar
1 Tbsp soy sauce
1 tsp ginger minced
1 tsp garlic minced
½ tsp salt

Instructions

1. Rinse chicken wings and dry them with a paper towel. Place them in a large bowl and season with garlic powder, onion powder, and ½ tsp salt.
2. Cover the chicken with corn starch and using kitchen tongs to stir, make sure that all chicken pieces are coated. Tap each piece on the side of the bowl (to remove excess starch) and place it in the Instant Pot Duo Crisp Air Fryer basket.
3. Close the lid of the basket and choose the Air Fry option. Cook the chicken wings at 390°F for 30 minutes, turning and rotating chicken about every 10 minutes.

Korean Air Fried Chicken Sauce

1. Add the sauce ingredients into a small saucepan over medium heat and whisk until they are combined. Bring the sauce to a boil and reduce the heat to low, simmer for 5 minutes. Remove it from heat and set it aside.
2. Once the chicken is done the cooking, add sauce to the wings and toss to cover all wings.

Nutrition Facts Per Serving

Calories 439, Total Fat 19g, Total Carbs 44g, Protein 23g

Air Fryer Crab Cakes

Prep time: 10 minutes, cook time: 10 minutes; Serves 4

9 Ingredients

8 Oz lump crab
1/4 cup red bell pepper chopped
2 green onion chopped
2 Tbsp mayonnaise
2 Tbsp bread crumbs
1 Tbsp Dijon mustard
1 tsp old bay seasoning
Oil for spraying
Squeeze of lemon

Instructions

1. In a bowl, place the red bell pepper, dijon mustard, old bay, green onion, bread crumbs, mayonnaise and stir until combined.
2. Form 4 patties with the mixture.
3. Place the patties on the tray in the Instant Pot Duo Crisp Air Fryer basket and lightly spray with oil. Close the lid of the Air Fryer.
4. Choose the Air Fry option and cook at 370°F for 10 minutes. Squeeze some lemon over the tops before serving.

Nutrition Facts Per Serving

Calories 122, Total Fat 6g, Total Carbs 5g, Protein 12g

French Fries

Prep time: 5 minutes, cook time: 22 minutes; Serves 4

2 Ingredients

1-3 medium-sized russet potatoes cut into 1/2 inch fries
2 Tbsp olive oil

Instructions

1. Soak the potatoes in a bowl of water for one hour.
2. Drain the potatoes and dry them with a paper towel. Then, place the potatoes in a dry bowl and add oil.
3. Choose the Air Fry option and set the Instant Pot Duo Crisp Air Fryer to 400°F. Close the Instant Pot Duo Crisp Air Fryer lid and Air fry for 22-30 minutes. Shake the Air Fryer basket or stir the ingredients every 5 minutes for uniform cooking.

Nutrition Facts Per Serving

Calories 107, Total Fat 7g, Total Carbs 10g, Protein 1g

Chapter 8 Desserts

Banana Bread

Prep time: 20 minutes, cook time: 35 minutes; Serves 4

11 Ingredients
1/2 cup all-purpose flour
1/4 cup wheat germ or whole-wheat flour
1/2 teaspoon kosher salt
1/4 teaspoon baking soda
2 ripe bananas
1/2 cup granulated sugar
1/4 cup vegetable oil
1/4 cup plain yogurt (not Greek)
1/2 teaspoon pure vanilla extract
1 large egg
1 to 2 tablespoons turbinado sugar, optional

Instructions

1. Whisk together flour, wheat germ, salt and baking soda in medium bowl. Mash the bananas until very smooth in a separate medium bowl. Add granulated sugar, oil, yogurt, vanilla and egg to the banana and whisk until smooth. Sift the dry ingredients over the wet and fold together with a spatula until just combined. Scrape batter into a 7-inch round air fryer insert, metal cake pan or foil pan and smooth the top. Sprinkle the top of the batter with the turbinado sugar if desired, for a crunchy, sweet topping.
2. Put the pan in the Instant Pot Duo Crisp Air Fryer and close the lid. Select the Air Fry option and cook at 310°F, turning the pan halfway through, until a toothpick inserted in the middle of the bread comes out clean for 30 to 35 minutes. Transfer the pan to a rack to cool for 10 minutes. Unmold the banana bread from the pan and let cool completely on a rack before slicing into wedges to serve.

Nutrition Facts Per Serving
Calories 400, Total Fat 16g, Total Carbs 57g, Protein 7g

Air Fryer Brownies

Prep time: 5 minutes, cook time: 15 minutes; Serves 4

9 Ingredients

½ cup all-purpose flour
6 Tbsp unsweetened cocoa powder
¾ cup of sugar
¼ cup unsalted butter melted
2 large eggs
1 Tbsp vegetable oil
½ tsp vanilla extract
¼ tsp salt
¼ tsp baking powder

Instructions

1. Grease a 7-inch baking pan with butter on the bottom and all sides.
2. Choose the Bake option on the Instant Pot Duo Crisp Air Fryer and set the temperature to 330°F. Press start and let it preheat for 5 minutes.
3. Take a large bowl and stir the all-purpose flour, cocoa powder, sugar, butter, eggs, vegetable oil, vanilla extract, salt, and baking powder thoroughly.
4. Add it to the prepared baking pan and smooth out the top.
5. Once preheated, place in the preheated Instant Pot Duo Crisp Air Fryer basket and bake for 15 minutes, check if it is properly baked by running a toothpick through it, it should come clean.
6. Allow cooling in the pan before removing and cutting.

Nutrition Facts Per Serving

Calories 402, Total Fat 18g, Total Carbs 54g, Protein 6g

Air Fried Cinnamon Rolls

Prep time: 20 minutes, cook time: 9 minutes; Serves 8

8 Ingredients
1 Pound frozen bread dough, thawed
¼ Cup butter, melted and cooled
¾ Cup brown sugar
1½ Tsp ground cinnamon
4 Oz cream cheese softened
2 Tbsp butter softened
1¼ Cups powdered sugar
½ Tbsp vanilla

Instructions
1. Bring the bread dough to room temperature. Over a lightly floured surface, roll up the dough to a thirteen-inch by 11-inch rectangle. Position the rectangle so the thirteen-inch side, so that it is facing you. Brush the liquid or melted butter over the dough, leaving one-inch border uncovered along the edge farthest away from you.
2. Mix the brown sugar and cinnamon in a little bowl.
3. Sprinkle the mixture over the buttered dough, keeping one-inch border uncovered. Start with the closest edge and roll the dough into a log by starting with the closest edge to you. Tightly roll the dough, and make sure to evenly roll and then push out any air pockets. When you reach the uncovered edge of the dough, press the dough onto the roll and seal it together.
4. Cut the log into eight pieces, slicing it slowly with a sawing motion so you don't flatten the dough. Turn the slices on the sides and then cover it with a clean towel. Place the rolls in the hottest part of the kitchen for 1 to 2 hours to rise.
5. For making the glaze, place the butter and cream cheese in a microwave-safe bowl. Soften the mixture in the microwave until it is easy to stir (30 sec). Gradually add the powdered sugar and stir it to combine. Add the vanilla extract and whisk it until smoothens. Set it aside.
6. After the rise of the rolls, preheat the Instant Pot Duo Crisp Air Fryer at 350ºF.
7. Transfer four of the rolls to the Instant Pot Duo Crisp Air Fryer Basket.
8. Close the Air Fryer lid and cook for about 5 minutes.
9. Turn the rolls over and again air fry them for another 4 minutes. Repeat the steps with the remaining four rolls.
10. Cooldown the rolls for a few minutes before glazing. Then spread large dollops of cream cheese glaze on top of the hot cinnamon rolls, and then allow some of the glaze to drip down the side of the rolls.

Nutrition Facts Per Serving
Calories 391, Total Fat 15g, Total Carbs 60g, Protein 4g

Marshmallow and Chocolate Sandwiched Graham Cracker

Prep time: 5 minutes, cook time: 5 minutes; Serves 2

3 Ingredients

2 Graham Crackers broken in half
2 marshmallows broken in half
2 small pieces of chocolate

Instructions

1. Place the Graham cracker halves on the tray of Instant Pot Duo Crisp Air Fryer.
2. Take the sticky side of the broken marshmallow and place it on the Graham Cracker, push it so that it sticks to the cracker.
3. Close the Air Fryer lid and cook on 390°F for 5 to 7 minutes, or until the tops of the marshmallows get a nice golden color.
4. Once this is done, add a piece of chocolate on top of the marshmallows, then put the other half of the graham cracker over it.

Nutrition Facts Per Serving

Calories 245, Total Fat 13g, Total Carbs 29g, Protein 3g

Cookies and Cream Cheesecake

Prep time: 15 minutes, cook time: 40 minutes; Serves 6

8 Ingredients:
1 cup Water
2 tbsp unsalted butter melted
1 tsp vanilla extract
1/2 cup full-fat sour cream
1/2 cup granulated sugar
16 oz cream cheese softened
26 cream-filled chocolate sandwich cookies divided
2 large eggs room temperature

Instructions
1. Grease 7 inch push pan and set it aside.
2. Place 16 chocolate cookies in a zip-lock bag and seal it. With a rolling pin roll it until crumbs are formed.
3. Take a small bowl then mix the crushed cookies and the melted butter together.
4. Press the cookie crust into the bottom and halfway up sides of the greased Push Pan. Place the pan in the freezer till you prepare the cheesecake batter.
5. With an electric mixer, cream together cream cheese, sugar, and vanilla. Beat it for around 2 minutes until it is light and fluffy.
6. Slowly mix in the sour cream.
7. Add the eggs - one at a time, beating after each addition. Only mix until it is combined. Do not overmix.
8. Chop remaining cookies and fold half of them into the cheesecake batter. Reserve remaining chopped cookies for topping.
9. Choose the Bake option from the Instant Pot Duo Crisp Air Fryer settings and push the start button after setting the temperature to 360°F.
10. Pour batter into the push pan. Once preheated, put the pan on the tray of the Air Fryer.
11. Close the Air Fryer lid and bake for 40 minutes.
12. When the timer beeps, unlock the lid and remove it.
13. Carefully remove the pan from Air Fryer Tray. Place on a cooling rack and let cool to room temperature.
14. Cover it with a plastic wrap and refrigerate for 8 hours minimum.
15. Top the cheesecake with the remaining cookies crumbs and serve.

Nutrition Facts Per Serving
Calories 660, Total Fat 44g, Total Carbs 56g, Protein 10g

Blueberry Almond Mason Jar Cakes

Prep time: 5 minutes, cook time: 15 minutes; Serves 4

8 Ingredients:
4 large eggs
2 tsp pure vanilla extract
1/4 tsp salt
1 cup blueberries
1 tsp baking powder
1/4 cup erythritol
1/4 cup sliced almonds
1 1/3 cups almond flour

Instructions
1. Take a bowl and whisk eggs and vanilla extract. Add flour, erythritol, baking powder, and salt, then stir to combine. Fold in the blueberries.
2. Spray four 6 ounce Mason jars with cooking oil. Divide the batter into the jars, top each jar with some of the almonds, and cover them with an aluminum foil.
3. Pour 1 cup. Put the jars in the Instant Pot Duo Crisp Air Fryer tray. Close the lid.
4. Press the Bake button before adjusting the time to 15 minutes.
5. When you hear the timer beep, unlock the lid.
6. Carefully remove the Mason jars from the inner pot and allow it to cool before serving.

Nutrition Facts Per Serving
Calories 410, Total Fat 26g, Total Carbs 28g, Protein 16g